Questions and Answers

MODERN WORLD
HISTORY

Greg Lacey History Officer
Colin Shephard Chief Examiner

SERIES EDITOR: BOB McDUELL

Letts
EDUCATIONAL

Contents

HOW TO USE THIS BOOK	1
ASSESSMENT OBJECTIVES IN HISTORY	2
SUMMARY OF ADVICE ON USING SOURCES	4
EXAMINATION TECHNIQUE	4

QUESTIONS AND REVISION SUMMARIES

1	The First World War, 1914–18	5
2	The Peace Treaties of 1919–20 and the League of Nations	10
3	Germany, 1919–39	15
4	Russia, 1917–41	20
5	The United States of America, 1919–41	25
6	Events in the 1930s leading to the Second World War	31
7	The Cold War	33

ANSWERS	38

Introduction

HOW TO USE THIS BOOK

The aim of this book is to help you to achieve a good grade in your GCSE Modern World History examination. It has been written to give you practice in answering the kinds of questions that the examination will include. To do this successfully you need to know what qualities the examiners are looking for in students' answers. This book includes many examples of questions from past examinations, answers and marking schemes. As you work through the questions, write your answers down on a piece of paper. When you have completed a question, turn to the Answers Section and compare your answer with the examples and Examiner's tips given. This will define the strengths and weaknesses of the approach you have taken. Once you have covered all the topics in this way, you should understand exactly what the examination will demand of you.

To use this book as effectively as possible it is important that you have information on the particular syllabus that you are studying at school. There are several GCSE Modern World History syllabuses; all have many features in common, but are also different in important respects. They include different choices of topics, and differ in the ways in which these topics are examined. Each of the following examining groups has its own syllabus:

- Midland Examining Group (MEG)
- Northern Examinations and Assessment Board (NEAB)
- Southern Examining Group (SEG)
- University of London Examinations and Assessment Council (ULEAC)
- Welsh Joint Education Committee (WJEC)
- International General Certificate of Secondary Education (IGCSE)

You need to know which of the above syllabuses you are studying, and which topics within the syllabus your teacher has chosen to cover. You will then know which sections in this book you should concentrate upon.

The book includes examples of questions on the most popular topics in GCSE Modern World History. It is therefore likely that most, if not all, of the topics you have studied in class will be covered. The material is organized topic by topic, so that as you cover a topic in class, or in your revision, you can refer to the relevant section in this book, gaining valuable experience in practising your historical skills on real questions from previous years' examinations.

Even though many of the questions will not be taken from the syllabus you are studying, the material will still be valid, as the **assessment objectives** (that is, the knowledge, skills, and historical understanding being tested) are the same for all GCSE History syllabuses. Nonetheless, as good revision technique, you should also obtain copies of past papers for the syllabus you are studying, so that you are thoroughly familiar with the exact combination of topics, questions and assessment objectives you will face in the examination.

Each topic covered by this book includes the following elements:

1 A revision summary – a brief statement of the events included within the topic.
2 Past examination questions – which test different assessment objectives, such as your ability to interpret historical sources or show your understanding of what caused certain events to happen.
3 Specimen answers and Examiner's tips – which provide an analysis of the strengths and weaknesses of an answer, with indications of how marks can be earned.

History is not one of those subjects where, in general, the examiners are just looking for correct factual knowledge. They are concerned with how you *use* your knowledge to construct historical explanations and to deal with historical sources. This book, then, is not intended to teach you the facts about the events you have studied – you can revise these from your class notes and textbooks. Instead, each section of this book will show you how to make the best use of what you already know, in order to do as well as you can in the examination.

Introduction

ASSESSMENT OBJECTIVES IN HISTORY

Assessment objectives are the qualities which are tested in the examination. There are four assessment objectives which are common to all syllabuses in Modern World History, but most syllabuses test only three of these in the written examination. The wording of the assessment objectives in the following descriptions is that used by the Midland Examining Group (MEG), whose examination is used by the greatest number of schools. If you are studying another examining group's syllabus, the wording of the objectives may differ slightly, or the syllabus may list them in a different order. Do not worry about this, the objectives are essentially the same.

Objective 1: You should be able to recall, select and deploy relevant knowledge, and communicate in a clear and coherent form.
This is the objective which is concerned with your factual knowledge of the topics you have studied, and your ability to communicate that knowledge. In one sense, this is the most important objective of all, because without any factual knowledge you could not demonstrate any historical skills or understanding. Each of the other assessment objectives therefore depends on this one. However, *on its own*, this objective is not what GCSE History is really about. Few questions will test this objective alone because it is concerned only with the facts; no argument, no analysis, no explanation, no use of sources. Of course, some questions in history are about the facts ('In which year did the First World War end?', 'What was the New Economic Policy?'). However, since factual knowledge is bound to be present in answers which relate to all of the other objectives, why test it on its own? Most of the examining groups regard Objective 1 as an *enabling* objective – something which helps you show your ability on the other objectives – rather than as an end in itself. You need factual knowledge, and the more detailed and accurate your knowledge the better, but do not expect to see many questions which test knowledge alone.

Objective 2: You should be able to demonstrate understanding of historical terminology and concepts (cause and consequence, change and continuity, similarity and difference).
The importance of this objective is that it tests your ability to analyse and construct explanations of historical events and developments. In GCSE History examinations you will not often be asked 'What happened...?'. Instead the questions might explore 'Why did it happen?', 'Was it important?', 'Did it change everything/something/anything?'. These are not the kinds of questions to which answers will be correct or incorrect, because they involve opinions – *your* opinions. This does not mean that you can simply write down anything which occurs to you. For your opinions to have any value, they must be supported by valid historical examples (which is where your knowledge of the events comes in). Objective 2 spells out certain concepts you will have to use in constructing different types of historical explanations. Questions in the examination will target one or other of these concepts to test the level of understanding you can demonstrate in constructing your answer. Let's take the example of the Treaty of Versailles to show how different questions can test your understanding of different concepts.

- 'Why did the Allies make such a harsh treaty with Germany in 1919?' (*cause*)
- 'How successful was the Treaty of Versailles? Explain your answer.' (*consequence*)
- 'Was Germany still a great power after the Treaty of Versailles? Explain your answer.' (*change/continuity*)

In answering these questions you must give an explanation. Later in the book you will find many examples of how to do this. Here it is enough to say that it matters much less *what* your explanation is, than *how* you go about constructing it. The examiner has no right answer in mind; what counts is the quality of thought that goes into your answer, and your ability to support thoughts with accurate and relevant historical examples. Learn to recognize Objective 2 questions. They differ from Objective 1 in requiring analysis or explanation, rather than description and factual recall. As we shall see, they differ from Objective 4 in not requiring you to use historical sources to answer the question.

Introduction

Objective 3: You should be able to reveal empathy with individuals and societies in their historical setting.
This objective is to do with understanding the thoughts, motives and beliefs of people who lived in the past, i.e. the ability to view historical events from the perspectives of people alive at the time. Most of the examining groups do not test this objective in the written examination papers, preferring to include it as an assessment objective in course work. It is not, therefore, an objective which will be covered in detail in this book. However, even when empathy is not being directly tested, it can still be used in answers to questions testing other objectives, particularly those dealing with causation in Objective 2. In explaining why something happened it can be relevant to include the motives, intentions and beliefs of people involved in the events. If you can use empathy relevantly in answers to Objective 2 questions, you will be credited for doing so.

Objective 4: You should be able to interpret and evaluate a wide range of historical sources, and their use as evidence.
This is the objective which tests your ability to use the 'raw materials' of history – the sources. You can always tell when Objective 4 is being tested; just ask yourself, 'Could I answer this question if the source(s) were not there?' If the answer is 'Yes', then it is not an Objective 4 question. Watch out for 'stimulus material' questions. These include sources, but only to give you information to use in your answer. You are not required to interpret or evaluate the stimulus material. Such questions are used to test Objectives 1 and 2, but not Objective 4.

Objective 4, then, is testing your ability to *interpret* and *evaluate* historical sources. What is the difference between these two abilities? Interpreting a source is the process of understanding what it tells you. This might not be immediately obvious. Take the following telegram sent by the British Prime Minister, Lloyd George, to Field Marshal Haig, British Commander-in-Chief in France, on 16 October, 1917:

> *'The War Cabinet desires to congratulate you upon the achievements of the British armies in the great battle which has been raging since 31st July.... You and your men have driven the enemy back with skill and courage and have filled the enemy with alarm. I am personally glad to pass this message to you, and to your gallant troops, and to state again my confidence in your leadership.'*

If asked what this source tells us about progress made by British armies in the 3rd Battle of Ypres during the First World War, we might jump to the conclusion that they were doing well. If we just believed what the source says, or if we knew nothing about this topic, we would not realize that it refers to an offensive which became impossibly bogged down in the mud of Flanders, achieved almost nothing and saw the deaths of around half a million men (of whom, approximately, half were British). To interpret this source, then, we have to use our knowledge of the topic, which will lead us to realize that during wartime the Prime Minister must support the country's armed forces, and cannot afford openly to admit that things are going badly. In this light, the source is not a literal statement of the truth, but an official message of encouragement and support. Interpretation is all about understanding the real *meaning* of a source, and not just taking what it says at face value.

Evaluation takes the process of interpretation a step further, by asking what *use* we can make of a source in finding out about the past. So the above telegram is not much use at all as evidence about the progress of the 3rd Battle of Ypres, in fact it is positively misleading for that purpose, but it could be much more useful as evidence of how British politicians tried to hide the reality of the war in order to maintain morale.

Questions on Objective 4 can be very varied in type. The following is a list of skills which you might be expected to demonstrate:

1 comprehension of sources
2 location and extraction of relevant information from the sources
3 distinguishing between facts and opinions
4 indicating deficiencies in sources, such as gaps and inconsistencies

Introduction

5 detecting bias
6 comparing and contrasting sources
7 reaching conclusions based on the use of sources as evidence.

You will find examples of questions testing most of these in this book, along with detailed advice on how to answer them. But remember, when answering Objective 4 questions *never* judge a source solely by its type – whether a photograph, a cartoon, an eye-witness account, a newspaper article, etc. **Always** look at what the source actually tells you, and judge its reliability in relation to your knowledge of the topic. The weakest answers to Objective 4 questions are always those that rely on generalizations, e.g. 'He was an eyewitness, he must know what happened' or 'Primary sources are more reliable than secondary sources', and ignore what the source itself actually says or shows.

SUMMARY OF ADVICE ON USING SOURCES

> The following five simple rules should help you to improve your answer to almost all source-based questions:
>
> 1   Never be satisfied with judging the reliability or usefulness of a source by its **type**.
> 2   Always use the **content** of a source in your answer.
> 3   Do not take sources at face-value. Look beneath the surface of the source to what you can infer from it – think about what the source really means, rather than just what it says.
> 4   Do not automatically believe a source; always try to **check** what it says.
> 5   Always use your **knowledge of the topic** to help you judge the reliability or usefulness of a source.

EXAMINATION TECHNIQUE

No book, however useful, will enable you to achieve a high grade if you have poor examination technique. In every examination you take, keep the following pieces of advice in mind:

1 Read the questions carefully. Where there is a choice of questions, make sure you have read all the questions you could answer, and that you have chosen those you can answer best.
2 Answer the right number of questions, and complete each question. Obey all the instructions to candidates, such as answering questions from different sections of the paper.
3 Manage the time you have available effectively. Split the time sensibly between the questions you have to answer. There is little point writing an enormous amount on a topic you know well, only to fail to complete your last question. All the marks on questions you do not answer are marks lost to you, so finish the examination, even if it means cutting some answers shorter than you might wish.
4 The question paper shows how many marks are available on each question. Use this as a guide to the amount of time you spend on each question. Do not write lengthy answers to questions which carry few marks.
5 Answer the question as it is asked, and not how you might wish it to be. The most common fault in examination technique is irrelevance. Marks are *only* given for answers that do what the question asks.
6 In History examinations you are expected to produce ideas, arguments, explanations. It is important to support these with relevant examples. Never make unsupported assertions.
7 Remember that marks will be awarded for accurate spelling, punctuation and grammar. Check through your work carefully at the end of the examination and correct any errors.

The First World War, 1914–18

1 THE OUTBREAK OF WAR

REVISION SUMMARY

- On 28 June 1914, a Serbian student, Gavrilo Princip, shot dead Archduke Franz Ferdinand, heir to the Austro-Hungarian empire. The shooting took place in Sarajevo, the capital of Bosnia. Bosnia was part of the huge Austro-Hungarian empire. The neighbouring country of Serbia thought that Bosnia should be joined to Serbia, especially as there were many Serbs living in Bosnia.

- On 23 July, Austria-Hungary made a series of demands to the Serbian government. When Serbia failed to agree to all of the demands, Austria-Hungary declared war on Serbia on 28 July.

- The alliance system, at that time, meant that all the major powers were dragged into the war. Germany and Austria led one group; Britain, France and Russia the other. When Russia prepared to help Serbia, Germany declared war on Russia on 1 August. Then, on 3 August, Germany declared war on France. On 4 August, when Germany invaded Belgium, Britain declared war on Germany.

- Germany and Britain had long been rivals. They had been competing to build the most powerful navy to win control of the seas.

- Germany was worried about its frontiers with France and Russia. If both countries attacked Germany at the same time, the German army would have to fight on two fronts. In 1897 General Schlieffen had worked out a plan to avoid this. Germany would first attack France through neutral Belgium. France would be quickly defeated. The German army would then turn east to fight Russia.

- The Schlieffen Plan nearly worked. The German army quickly marched through northern France and by September had reached the River Marne, within sight of Paris. At the Battle of the Marne, the French and the small British Expeditionary Force stopped the German advance. Another important factor was the Russian victories on the eastern front, which led to Germany having to send more troops to the east, thus weakening its effort against France.

2 THE WESTERN FRONT

- Everybody had expected the war to be over by Christmas 1914. But it was not to be. Both sides now dug a network of trenches. By the end of 1914 the trenches stretched from the English Channel to Switzerland. The trenches were protected by barbed wire and machine guns. The land between the two sets of trenches was called 'No man's land'.

- The situation on the western front was one of stalemate, with neither side being strong enough to defeat the other. The conditions in the trenches were dreadful. The generals on both sides (from 1915 the British commander was Haig) tried to smash the enemy by sheer weight of numbers, but hundreds of thousands of soldiers were mown down by enemy fire as they attacked across 'No man's land'.

- In 1916 the Germans launched an offensive against the French at Verdun. Later in 1916 the British attacked on the Somme. In the Battle of the Somme there were more than 1 million casualties. Both battles ended in stalemate.

3 OTHER FRONTS

- The fighting on the eastern front between Russia and Germany also developed into a stalemate and produced many casualties. The war was fought in many other parts of the world too – in Italy, Turkey, Palestine, Africa and China.

- In 1915 Winston Churchill, the First Lord of the Admiralty, tried to break the deadlock by planning an attack on Turkey on the Gallipoli peninsula. But due to poor planning, the troops were pinned down on the beaches. At the beginning of 1916 they were withdrawn.

1 The First World War, 1914–18

REVISION SUMMARY

4 THE WAR AT SEA AND IN THE AIR

- There was also stalemate at sea. Both sides kept their large fleets in harbour. The Battle of Jutland, 1916, was the only major naval battle. The British lost most ships, but the German fleet did not leave its harbour again.
- Submarines were used by the Germans to sink merchant ships bringing food to Britain. But this threat was largely overcome by the use of convoys.
- At first, both sides had only a handful of reconnaissance aircraft. Soon, fighter aircraft and bombers were developed, although they did not play a major role. The Germans used Zeppelin airships to bomb enemy towns.

5 THE HOME FRONT

- Everybody, even people in Britain, was affected by the war. There were food shortages, factories had to manufacture munitions and some major cities were bombed.
- At first, the British government relied on men volunteering for the armed forces. But the enormous casualty figures made it necessary to introduce conscription in 1916.
- With so many men needed for the fighting, many women in Britain took on new types of work in factories, on farms, driving trains and buses. Shortly before the war ended, women over the age of 30 were given the vote.

6 THE END OF THE WAR

If you need to revise this subject more thoroughly, see the relevant topics in the Letts GCSE World History Study Guide.

- In 1917 the USA declared war on Germany. It was hoped that the American troops might break the stalemate on the western front. Before this could happen the new Communist government in Russia made peace with Germany. This gave Germany extra troops for the western front and in the spring of 1918 they launched a huge attack.
- The Allies managed to hold on. By the early summer, large numbers of American troops were arriving in Europe. In July the Allies launched a counterattack. Large numbers of tanks were used in the attack. The German army was gradually pushed back.
- By the autumn it was clear that Germany was losing the war. On 11 November an armistice was signed and the war was at an end. Germany and its allies had been defeated.

The First World War, 1914–18

QUESTIONS

1 Study carefully Sources A to E which refer to recruitment to the British armed forces. Then answer **all** the questions.

SOURCE A

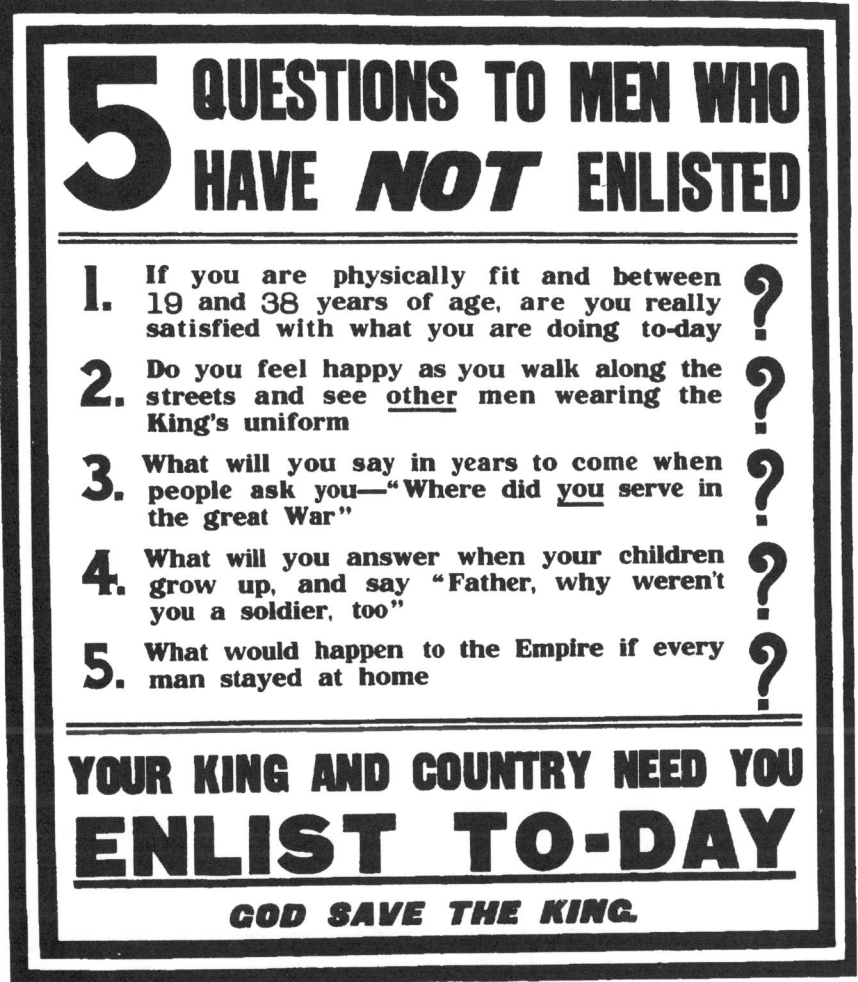

A British recruiting poster issued in 1914.

SOURCE B

Extracts from the diary of an Essex clergyman, the Reverend Andrew Clark

1 May 1915: William Milton, foremen of Lyons Hall farm, does not approve of all the recruiting posters on tree trunks and walls. 'If the government want more men let them take idlers not workmen. Unless the war is over before August there will not be enough men for the harvest.' The men say 'We will go when we like, or when we are ordered.' Conscription, being just, would be welcome.

9 May 1915: The annoyance of farm labourers with the recruitment campaign is shown by the fact that every recruiting poster has been torn down.

1 The First World War, 1914–18

QUESTIONS

SOURCE C

Army recruiting figures, August 1914 to December 1915. The figures were published in 1923.

1914: August 300,000; September 450,000; October 137,000; November 170,000; December 117,000

1915: January 156,000; February 88,000; March 114,000; April 119,000; May 135,000; June 114,000; July 95,000; August 96,000; September 71,000; October 113,000; November 122,000; December 55,000

SOURCE D

Men of the St Helens (Lancashire) Pals' Battalion in February 1915. The photograph was printed in a local newspaper.

SOURCE E

An extract from King George V's 'Message to his people', 25 May 1916

To enable our country to organize more effectively its military resources, I have, acting on the advice of my ministers, agreed to the Military Service Bill.

I wish to express my thanks for the splendid patriotism and self sacrifice which my people have shown by voluntary enlistment since the start of the war. I am confident that they will endure this additional sacrifice.

The First World War, 1914–18

(a) Study Source D. What was a 'Pals' Battalion? (2)

(b) Study Source E. What changes to the system of recruitment were made by the Military Services Bill of May 1916? (2)

(c) Study Source C. In what ways might these figures be useful to an historian studying British recruitment in the First World War? Explain your answer. (6)

(d) Study Sources A and B. Which of these two sources gives the more reliable view of British attitudes to recruitment? Explain your answer. (8)

(e) Study all the sources. 'Conscription was introduced because voluntary recruitment was not working.' Do these sources provide reliable evidence to show this view to be true? Explain your answer carefully. (12)

MEG 1994

2 Study the poster below and then attempt **all** parts of the question.

A British poster, 1917.

(a) The poster points out the danger to Britain of German submarines. German submarines sank many ships carrying supplies to Britain. Was this the most serious way in which British civilians were affected by enemy action? Explain your answer. (10)

(b) The poster above is an example of propaganda. Propaganda was very widely used during the First World War. Why was this the case? (10)

(c) The poster has a woman as its central character. In what ways did women become increasingly important to the war effort? (10)

SEG 1992

2 The Peace Treaties of 1919–20 and the League of Nations

REVISION SUMMARY

1 INTRODUCTION

- On 11 November 1918 the First World War came to an end.
- The Great Powers on the victorious side – Britain, France, Italy and the United States – had to decide how the losers would be treated.
- Many people in the victorious countries wanted to take revenge on the losers.
- The cost of the war, both human and material, was huge. Around eight and a half million people were killed in the fighting. Many countries were almost bankrupted after the war.
- Even before the end of fighting, great changes were taking place in many countries. The Austro-Hungarian empire was disintegrating, as was the Ottoman (Turkish) empire. The Bolshevik Revolution in November 1917 took Russia into a period of civil war. In Germany itself the Kaiser abdicated in November 1918, and the country seemed on the brink of revolution.
- In January 1919 representatives of the victorious powers met in Paris to decide on the terms of the peace settlement. The major decisions were taken by the Prime Ministers of Britain and France, Lloyd George and Clemenceau, and President Wilson of the United States.
- In 1919–20 treaties between the victors and each of the defeated nations were signed:

    Treaty of Versailles (1919) with Germany
    Treaty of St Germain (1919) with Austria
    Treaty of Neuilly (1919) with Bulgaria
    Treaty of Trianon (1920) with Hungary
    Treaty of Sèvres (1920) with Turkey, later amended by the Treaty of Lausanne (1923)

2 THE TREATY OF VERSAILLES

- The French wanted Germany weakened so that it would never again be a threat to France. The British and Americans had doubts about this, but in the end agreed to punish Germany. The Germans were given no choice but to sign the treaty; they were not allowed to join in the negotiations.
- Germany lost territory in Europe, and had all its colonies taken away. The League of Nations took over the Saar and Danzig.
- The size of Germany's armed forces was strictly limited.
- Germany had to accept responsibility for the war ('war guilt') and agree to pay reparations.
- The Rhineland was demilitarized.
- The Treaty of Brest-Litovsk with Russia was made void, which enabled Poland, Estonia, Latvia and Lithuania to become independent states. Poland was given access to the Baltic Sea through the 'Polish Corridor'.
- The League of Nations was established.
- The treaty left many Germans feeling resentful at the treatment their country had received. Many non-Germans felt that it was foolish to treat Germany so harshly.

3 THE OTHER PEACE TREATIES

- The Austro-Hungarian empire was broken up, and new states established (Czechoslovakia, Austria, Hungary, Yugoslavia).
- *Anschluss* (union between Austria and Germany) was forbidden.
- Italy and Rumania received territory from the old Austro-Hungarian empire.
- Bulgaria lost territory to Yugoslavia and Greece.
- The Ottoman empire was broken up, with much of it being taken as League of Nations mandates.

The Peace Treaties of 1919–20 and the League of Nations

4 THE LEAGUE OF NATIONS

- The idea of an international organization to preserve world peace was included as one of President Wilson's '14 Points', the principles he had stated as a framework for ending the First World War.
- The League was established in the peace treaties of 1919–20. It was based in Geneva, Switzerland.
- The League consisted of the following organizations:

  1. The **Assembly** – all member states were represented in the Assembly, which discussed matters of international importance. Because all members had an equal vote, the Assembly did not have much power. The Great Powers dominated the League by being permanent members of the Council.
  2. The **Council** – this met more frequently than the Assembly, and was intended to cope with crises as they arose. Britain, France, Italy and Japan were permanent members. The Assembly voted for additional non-permanent members.
  3. The **Permanent Court of Justice** – this dealt with legal disputes between member states.
  4. The **Agencies** – the League set up a number of commissions to deal with a range of international problems such as mandates, health, refugees and labour.

5 WEAKNESSES OF THE LEAGUE

- Not all nations were members of the League. The USA was never a member, and of the Great Powers, only Britain and France were members throughout the life of the League.
- The League lacked the power to enforce its decisions. It had no army and relied on 'collective security' against aggressors. In practice, it could be ignored by powerful nations.
- As early as 1923, over the Corfu Incident, the League showed itself incapable of dealing with acts of aggression.
- The first major crisis for the League occurred when the Japanese invaded Manchuria in 1931. The League condemned Japan, but Japan simply withdrew from the League. Japanese aggression against China continued.
- The Italian invasion of Ethiopia was a disaster for the League. Although Italy was condemned and some sanctions put on it, the League failed to place sanctions on oil, which would have had some effect. Britain and France failed to give the League proper support. The League was powerless to prevent Italy completing the conquest of Ethiopia.

6 ACHIEVEMENTS OF THE LEAGUE

- The commissions of the League did much useful work.
- The League was successful in resolving some international disputes, e.g. the Aaland Islands dispute between Sweden and Finland, and the Greek attack on Bulgaria in 1925.
- During the 1920s membership of the League increased, notably with the inclusion of Germany from 1926.
- The League's existence gave opportunities for disputes to be solved by discussion rather than force.

REVISION SUMMARY

If you need to revise this subject more thoroughly, see the relevant topics in the *Letts* GCSE *World History Study Guide.*

2 The Peace Treaties of 1919–20 and the League of Nations

QUESTIONS

1 Many countries fought in the First World War. As a result, after the war ended in 1918, several peace treaties were signed. The following questions ask you about these treaties.

(a) (i) Name the treaty that was signed between the Allies and Austria in 1919. (1)

(ii) Explain was is meant by the phrase 'dictated settlement'. **Briefly** use your knowledge of the Treaty of Versailles to support your answer. (3)

(b) How **different** from each other were the following:

I   The Treaty of Sèvres, 1920;
II The Treaty of Lausanne, 1923? (6)

(c) 'The following two leaders were **very pleased** with the terms of the Treaty of Versailles:

I   Prime Minister Clemenceau of France;
II President Wilson of the USA.'

Do you agree with this statement? Explain your answer fully by referring to I, II **and** the terms of the Treaty of Versailles. (15)

MEG 1995

2 Study the sources below and then answer the questions which follow.

SOURCE A

Extract from a British newspaper, 27 November 1920

The first session of the Assembly of the League of Nations is a great landmark in the history of the world. As yet it is not complete in its composition. The United States, the founder of the idea, is strangely enough unrepresented, though it called the session. And Germany, Austria, Bulgaria and Turkey, of course, are as yet outside the League, while Russia also is not included.

SOURCE B

Extract from the Covenant of the League of Nations

The maintenance of peace requires the reduction of national armaments to the lowest point consistent with national safety.

The Peace Treaties of 1919–20 and the League of Nations

SOURCE C

From a British politician's diary, 1932

Everybody distrusts everybody. The major powers are against the League and determined to make disarmament fail. The French want more guarantees of security; the Germans are in confusion. Italy does not want to disarm except in the sense of being equally armed with France; no one is sure what Russia is doing; England's lack of leadership has infected the rest.

SOURCE D

Outline of the organization of the League of Nations

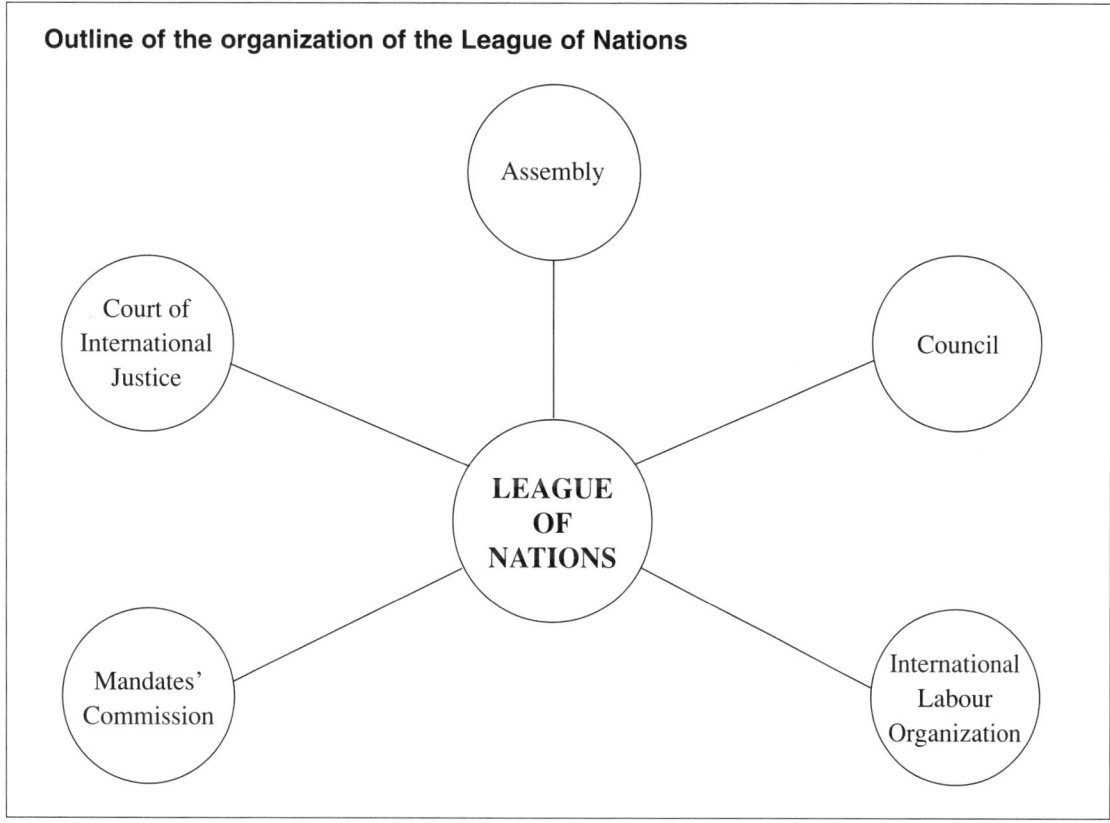

2. The Peace Treaties of 1919–20 and the League of Nations

QUESTIONS

SOURCE E

A British cartoon published in July 1935.

UPHILL WORK
John Bull: 'Even though it's only half a league,
it must go onward.'

(a) Name the city where the League of Nations had its headquarters. (1)

(b) Study Source A. How useful is this source for an historian writing about the setting up of the League of Nations? Use the source and your own knowledge to give reasons for your answer. (7)

(c) Do Sources B and C explain fully why the League of Nations failed to achieve disarmament? Use the sources and your own knowledge to give reasons for your answer. (7)

(d) An aim of the League of Nations was 'to encourage international cooperation'. Use Source D and your own knowledge to show how the League was organized to try and achieve this aim. (9)

(e) What does the cartoon in Source E tell an historian about the problems of the membership of the League of Nations? Use your own knowledge to support your answer. (6)

NEAB 1993

Germany, 1919–39

This chapter deals only with events inside Germany. It does not cover foreign policy.

REVISION SUMMARY

1 THE ESTABLISHMENT OF THE WEIMAR REPUBLIC

- By October 1918 it was clear that Germany would lose the First World War and would soon have to make peace.
- By the beginning of November, sailors and soldiers began to mutiny. There were calls for Kaiser William II to abdicate. Germany was on the brink of revolution.
- On 9 November, the Kaiser abdicated and the Republic was declared. On 11 November the armistice with the Allies was signed, and the war came to an end.
- These developments did not bring stability within Germany. Left-wing groups like the Spartacists tried to start a Communist revolution. They were crushed by the army and the *Freikorps* in January 1919.
- In January 1919 elections were held, and in February the National Assembly met in the town of Weimar (hence the 'Weimar Republic'). The Assembly produced a new constitution for Germany. Friedrich Ebert, leader of the Social Democrats (who had taken over the government on the Kaiser's abdication), became the first President of the Republic.

2 THE WEIMAR REPUBLIC

- The Republic survived until 1933. It faced many problems, but also had many successes.
- Many Germans blamed the Republic for the country's failure to win the First World War. They believed that Germany had not been defeated on the battlefield but had been 'stabbed in the back' by the politicians who signed the armistice. The Republic was also blamed for what Germans saw as the harsh terms of the Treaty of Versailles.
- There were a number of revolts by right-wing groups. The most famous of these was the Munich *Putsch* in 1923 led by Adolf Hitler. It was put down by the police and Hitler was sent to prison.
- The main problems faced by the Republic were economic. As a result of the Treaty of Versailles, Germany was faced with a bill of £6,600 million to be paid in instalments. Germany fell behind with the payments, following which France sent troops in 1923 to occupy the Ruhr, Germany's main coal and steel area. The government tried to make up for the lost production by printing money. This led to inflation. Soon the German mark was worthless.
- The economic recovery was led by Gustav Stresemann, who was Chancellor in 1923 and Foreign Minister until his death in 1929. In 1923 a new currency, called the Rentenmark, was introduced. The Dawes Plan of 1924 also helped. By this the Allies allowed Germany to pay the reparations in easier stages, and arranged for the withdrawal of French troops from the Ruhr. The USA lent Germany nearly $800 million. This money was invested in German industries which prospered. More goods were produced and unemployment fell.

3 THE DEPRESSION AND THE RISE OF HITLER

- Between 1924 and 1929 the Republic was a success. Most Germans accepted it and extremist parties such as Hitler's National Socialist (Nazi) party had little support.
- In 1929 the Wall Street stock market crashed. US investments in Germany were withdrawn. Many companies went bankrupt and by 1932 6 million Germans were unemployed.
- In this atmosphere of depression and poverty Hitler's National Socialist party increased its support. Since the failure of the *putsch* in 1923 and his release from prison the following year, Hitler had decided to use lawful means to gain power. In the elections in 1930 and 1932 Hitler attacked the economic and foreign policies of the Republic. He promised to cut the numbers of unemployed and to make Germany great again.

3 Germany, 1919–39

REVISION SUMMARY

- In the July 1932 elections the Nazis became the largest single party in the Reichstag, but they did not have an overall majority. In the November elections the Nazis lost some support but remained the largest party. President Hindenburg and his advisers thought that if Hitler was appointed Chancellor they would be able to control him. So on 30 January 1933 Hitler became Chancellor of a government of which there were only three Nazi members. He immediately demanded a new election.

4 HITLER BECOMES A DICTATOR

- In another election in March 1933 the Nazis still failed to win an overall majority, despite the SA and SS intimidating their opponents. Hitler now used intimidation to force the Reichstag to pass the Enabling Act. This allowed him to make laws without the consent of the Reichstag.
- The SA and the SS arrested political opponents, many of whom were sent to concentration camps. In July 1933 all political parties, except the Nazi Party, were banned. When Hindenburg died in 1934, Hitler gave himself a new title, *Führer* (leader).

5 LIFE IN NAZI GERMANY

- **Propaganda**. The Nazis kept control over the German people partly by terror. The Gestapo (secret state police) and the SS hunted down and removed Hitler's opponents. Joseph Goebbels, Minister of Propaganda, used the radio, the cinema and the press to spread Nazi ideas. Strict censorship made sure that opposing views were not seen or heard. Mass rallies were held.
- **Young people** were encouraged to join Nazi youth movements. Education was closely controlled. Girls were to be prepared for motherhood, while boys were to be ready to fight. They were taught that they were members of a master race and were encouraged to hate and despise Jews.
- **The Jews**. Hitler and many Germans believed that the Jews were responsible for many of Germany's troubles. Hitler regarded them as an inferior race, barely human. He thought they would corrupt the purity of the German race. In 1935 the Nuremberg Laws banned marriages between Jews and Germans. Jews also lost their German citizenship and their right to vote. In November 1938 during *Kristallnacht* (Crystal Night), thousands of Jewish shops were smashed and synagogues burned down; 40,000 Jews were rounded up and sent to concentration camps. Between 1941 and 1945 the Germans carried out the 'Final Solution' and murdered 6 million Jews in extermination camps, such as Auschwitz.
- **The German economy** was transformed by the Nazis. In 1936 they introduced the Four-year Plan. This included massive rearmament. Germany also aimed to become self-sufficient in essential raw materials, such as oil. The standard of living of the German people rose. The number of unemployed fell, wages rose and Germans began to afford consumer goods, such as cars. Large public works projects, such as the building of new motorways, provided some of the new jobs, but most were provided in factories making armaments.

If you need to revise this subject more thoroughly, see the relevant topics in the *Letts* GCSE *World History Study Guide*.

Germany, 1919–39

1 Study carefully Sources A to E which refer to economic problems in 1923 in Germany. Then answer **all** the questions.

SOURCE A

An account from a British book, published in 1985, which described the economic changes in Germany during 1923

By December 1922 the German government had stopped reparation payments. The French decided to go and get their money. In January 1923 French troops invaded Germany's most important coalmining and industrial area. The German government ordered workers and officials not to cooperate with the French. Now Germany had to import coal from abroad and support the workers who were resisting the French. The government's income fell and its spending rose. The German government printed more banknotes.

SOURCE B

A table showing food prices (in Reichsmarks), 1918–23

Commodity	1918	1922	August 1923	November 1923
1 egg	0.25	180	5,000	80,000,000
500g butter	3.00	2,400	150,000	6,000,000,000
1 kg bread	0.53	163	69,000	201,000,000

SOURCE C

The photograph shows middleclass women selling tin cans to raise money in 1923.

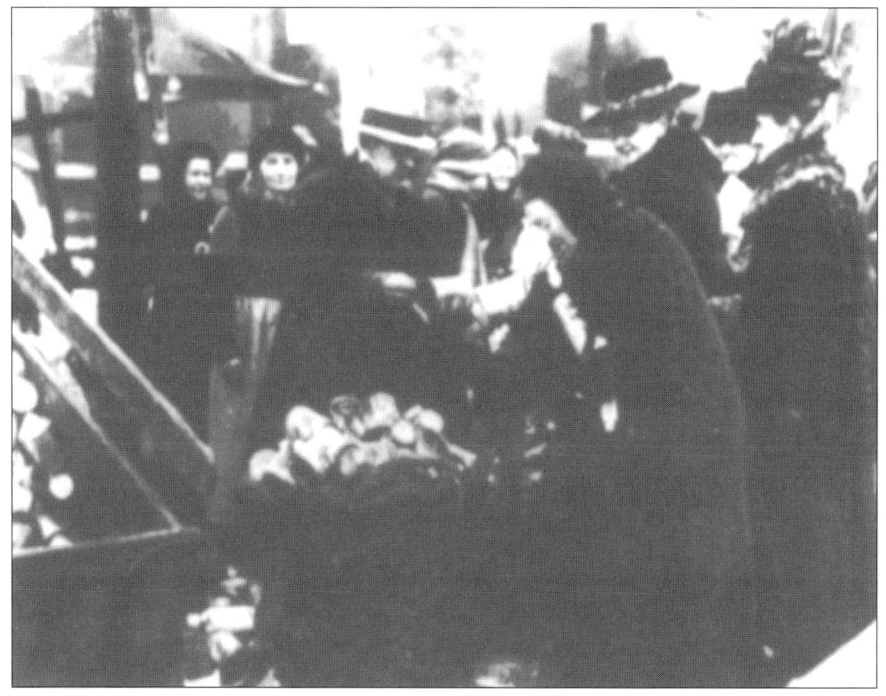

3 Germany, 1919–39

QUESTIONS

SOURCE D

A middleclass housewife later recalled her experience of hyperinflation in 1923

My husband set up his practice as an eye surgeon. My own income was fixed at 30,000 marks. However, 80 per cent of my husband's patients paid their fees three months after the treatment. We were virtually without any income. My brother-in-law owned a factory and, like all businessmen, was well off. His wife and I had our babies within a few days of each other and I remember how I was lying in a borrowed iron bedstead with my baby in a borrowed cradle, while she had everything for herself and her baby in pure silk. And yet we both came from the same sort of family background.

SOURCE E

A comment on the effects of the hyperinflation of 1923 written many years after the events described

As soon as factory gates opened and the workers streamed out, pay packets (often in old cigar boxes) in their hands, their wives grabbed the money, and rushed to the nearest shops to buy food before prices went up again. Salaries always lagged behind. People living on fixed incomes sank into deeper poverty.

A familiar sight in the streets was of people carrying laundry baskets full of paper money. It sometimes happened that thieves stole the baskets, but tipped out the money and left it on the spot.

(a) Study Source A. Give the name of:

  (i) 'Germany's most important coalmining and industrial area'; (1)

  (ii) the country which acted with France in this invasion. (1)

(b) Study Source C. Give two reasons why Germany's middle classes were affected by the hyperinflation of 1923. (2)

(c) Study Source B. In what ways might this source be useful to an historian studying Weimar Germany? Explain your answer. (6)

(d) Study Source D and Source E. Which of these two sources gives the more reliable account of the effects of hyperinflation in Germany in 1923? Explain your answer. (8)

(e) Study all the sources. 'The economic crisis of 1923 brought equal suffering to all sections of the German people.' Do these sources provide reliable evidence to show this view to be true? Explain your answer carefully. (12)

MEG 1994

Germany, 1919–39

2 (a) Study this photograph taken in Berlin in the early 1930s, and then answer the questions (i) to (v) which follow: The sign translated reads 'Germans, do not buy from Jews'.

(i) Write a sentence explaining what National Socialists meant by the word 'Aryan'. (2)

(ii) Write a sentence explaining what is meant by 'antisemitism'. (2)

(iii) Write one or two sentences explaining why there was so much antisemitism in Germany during the 1930s. (3)

(iv) Write one or two sentences explaining why German Jews found it difficult to combat antisemitism. (3)

(v) Write a paragraph describing the measures that were taken against Jews in Germany during the years 1933–9. (5)

(b) **ESSAY QUESTION**

How successful were the domestic policies of the German government in the years 1933–9? (15)

ULEAC 1991

4 Russia, 1917–41

REVISION SUMMARY

This chapter deals only with events inside Russia (known from 1923 onwards as the Soviet Union). It does not deal with foreign policy.

1 INTRODUCTION
- From 1894 Russia was ruled by Tsar Nicholas II, who was weak and ineffective.
- Russia was an autocracy – a country in which the Tsar was absolute ruler and the people had little freedom.
- Russia was a poor country. By the early twentieth century industry was beginning to develop, but living conditions in the towns were very bad and in the countryside few of the peasants owned their own land.
- Opposition to the Tsar was growing. Many revolutionary groups wanted to overthrow the Tsar. More moderate opponents wanted social and political reform.
- Defeat in the war against Japan (1904–5) sparked off the 1905 revolution in Russia. The Tsar survived this, but had to grant some reforms, including allowing the Duma (a parliament which had little power) to meet.
- By the outbreak of the First World War in 1914 none of Russia's problems had been solved. Russia joined in the war on the Allied side against Germany.

2 RUSSIA AND THE EFFECTS OF THE FIRST WORLD WAR BY 1917
- By early 1917 Russia's armies were near to defeat.
- The war effort caused great hardship for the civilian population of Russia.
- Tsar Nicholas II was losing control of events, particularly in Petrograd where food riots and strikes broke out.
- The Tsar was unpopular for refusing much needed reforms and because of the influence of his wife and favourites such as Rasputin (murdered in December 1916).

3 THE REVOLUTIONS OF 1917
Note: because of the old calendar in use in Russia at the time, the Revolutions of 1917 can be called either the February/October or the March/November Revolutions.
- The March Revolution led to the abdication of the Tsar.
- The Provisional Government took over, with Kerensky later emerging as leader.
- Also powerful were the 'Soviets', soldiers' and workers' councils, set up in many big cities.
- The Provisional Government stayed in the war and more defeats followed.
- Dissatisfaction with the Provisional Government grew. Revolutionaries, such as the Mensheviks and the Bolsheviks (led by Lenin), increased their influence in the Soviets and planned another revolution.
- In early November, the Bolsheviks' Red Guards seized power in Petrograd. Lenin claimed to be ruler of Russia; in fact, at first the Bolsheviks controlled only a few major cities.

Russia, 1917–41

REVISION SUMMARY

4 THE CIVIL WAR AND THE BOLSHEVIK CONSOLIDATION OF POWER, 1918–21

- Lenin had promised 'Peace, bread and land' to the Russian people.
- Peace was made with the Germans by the Treaty of Brest-Litovsk.
- The Bolsheviks introduced Communist rule and set about crushing all opposition.
- Civil War soon broke out. The 'Whites' (opponents of the Bolsheviks) fought against the Red Army, created by Trotsky. Foreign countries helped the Whites, but opposition to the Bolsheviks was never united.
- Lenin used War Communism to ensure the victory of the Red Army by 1921.
- In 1921 the Kronstadt Rising showed Lenin the dangers of continuing with War Communism. He introduced the New Economic Policy (NEP) to allow Russia to recover.

5 STALIN'S RISE TO POWER

- In 1924 Lenin died. Trotsky and Stalin were his two possible successors.
- Trotsky, despite his fame and achievements, was disliked by the other Bolshevik leaders.
- Gradually Stalin, using the power built up in his time as Secretary of the Communist Party, increased his control.
- Trotsky was exiled in 1929. By then, Stalin had emerged as the new leader. Trotsky was eventually murdered, on Stalin's orders, in 1940.

6 STALIN'S RUSSIA

- Stalin proved to be a cruel and ruthless dictator, who transformed Russia into a modern state.
- He abolished the NEP and the state took control of all industry and agriculture.
- The first Five-Year Plan was introduced in 1928. This set production targets for heavy industry. Every five years a new plan set fresh targets. By the outbreak of war in 1941, Russia was a major industrial nation.
- In agriculture, the peasants were forced to work on huge new collective farms. Many peasants, particularly the better-off (called kulaks), resisted this change. Stalin crushed this resistance by force. Production in agriculture was slow to recover.
- Stalin destroyed all opposition. Throughout the 1930s his 'purges' led to the arrest, imprisonment and murder of millions of people, including most political and military leaders.

If you need to revise this subject more thoroughly, see the relevant topics in the *Letts* GCSE *World History Study Guide*.

4 Russia, 1917–41

QUESTIONS

1 (a) Study this passage, and then answer questions (i) to (v) which follow.

'On 12 March 1917, in Petrograd, demonstrators set fire to public buildings and attacked police stations and army barracks. That same day the Tsar abdicated. The March revolution – a leaderless movement – was over.'

(i) Write a sentence to explain what is meant by the word 'abdicated' as used in the passage. (2)

(ii) Write a sentence to explain the meaning of the word 'Duma'. (2)

(iii) Write one or two sentences to explain why people were demonstrating in Petrograd in March 1917. (3)

(iv) Write a paragraph to explain why the revolution was described as 'leaderless'. (4)

(v) Write a paragraph to explain why many people at the time blamed Tsar Nicholas for Russia's problems. (4)

(b) **ESSAY QUESTION**

'The Provisional Government was overthrown because it decided to continue fighting in the First World War.' Do you agree with this statement about the revolution of November 1917? Give reasons for your answer. (15)

ULEAC 1993

2 Study carefully Sources A–E which refer to the Purges during the 1930s. Then answer **all** the questions.

SOURCE A

> **An extract from a letter written by the local Communist Party Secretary to the secret police in Smolensk.**
>
> On 22 June 1936, a portrait of Trotsky was found in the home of Afanasiya Uromova. Uromova, it is said, is a corrupt member of the Kolkhoz. Vasili Ulyanov says that Uromova assaulted Ulyanov's father. I ask that Uromova be brought to trial.

Russia, 1917–41

SOURCE B

An extract from a novel published in 1940. The author, born in Hungary, was a journalist who had worked in the USSR writing for foreign newspapers.

Gletkin, a member of the secret police, is explaining the Purges to a prisoner. Gletkin said: 'In my village there is now the biggest steel-rail factory in the world. In the first year, the foremen would lie down to sleep when they should have been working. So they had to be shot. In all other countries the peasants had one or two hundred years to adapt to industry and machines. Here they had only ten years. If we didn't sack them or shoot them for every little mistake, no one would ever work.'

SOURCE C

A Soviet cartoon printed in 1937. It shows Trotsky washing blood from his hands.

4 Russia, 1917–41

QUESTIONS

SOURCE D

In a Soviet newsreel in 1937 Mikoyan, a member of the Politburo, praised the secret police.

We can honestly say that by working to uncover spies they have saved lives and protected us from enemies, spies and Trotskyists. These enemies organize train crashes, poison the food and water of the people and infect our cattle with disease. The secret police are led by a great Bolshevik.

SOURCE E

An extract from the memoirs of Lev Kopelev published in 1979. Kopelev was a Communist Party worker in the Ukraine in the 1920s and 30s. He was arrested in 1945 and spent ten years in prison camps.

We were taught, when we were young, that it was our duty to denounce friends and relatives. I never believed that Bukharin and Trotsky were Gestapo agents, and I was sure that Stalin never believed it either. But I believed Stalin was right in doing these terrible things, in order to make all those who opposed the Party look wrong. We were surrounded by enemies; we had to be united. Opposition leaders had to be presented as villains so that the people would hate them.

(a) Study Source D.

    (i) State what is meant by 'Bolshevik'. (1)

    (ii) What was the name of the secret police? (1)

(b) Study Source E. Give **two** 'enemies' which Communists felt were 'surrounding' them in the 1930s. (2)

(c) Study Source C. In what ways does this cartoon give a biased view of Trotsky? Explain your answer. (6)

(d) Study Source A and Source B. Which of these two sources gives the more reliable explanation for the purging of ordinary people in the 1930s? Explain your answer by referring to both sources. (8)

(e) Study **all** the sources.
'The Purges of the 1930s only took place because Stalin feared Trotsky.' Do these sources provide reliable evidence to show this view to be true? Explain your answer fully. (12)

MEG 1995

The United States of America, 1919–41

This chapter deals only with events inside the USA. It does not cover foreign policy.

REVISION SUMMARY

1 THE AMERICAN ECONOMY IN THE 1920s

- During the 1920s American industry experienced a 'boom', as production expanded rapidly.
- Consumer goods, such as radios, washing machines and cars, were produced in huge quantities, so that what had once been luxuries now became available to everybody.
- New ideas like hire purchase were used to encourage people to buy consumer goods.
- The US government believed in 'free enterprise', and involved itself as little as possible in the economy.
- Americans enjoyed the highest standard of living in the world.
- However, there were some economic problems. Agriculture was in trouble; overproduction and low prices were driving farmers out of business. By the late 1920s production in industry was slowing down, as the USA found it hard to sell its goods overseas.

2 AMERICAN SOCIETY IN THE 1920s AND 1930s

- The prosperity of the 1920s meant people had time and money for entertainment. Hollywood became the most important centre in the world for film production. Millions of people went to the cinema every week.
- The 'Roaring Twenties' saw great changes in social attitudes and fashions, particularly in the cities.
- In 1920 prohibition was introduced. This made the manufacture and sale of alcohol illegal. Gangsters took over the trade in alcohol, making enormous profits. The main effect of prohibition was to increase crime, and it was eventually repealed in 1933.
- Racism was a feature of American society, particularly in the south. The Ku Klux Klan flourished during these years.

3 THE WALL STREET CRASH AND THE GREAT DEPRESSION

- In October 1929 the New York Stock Exchange, known as 'Wall Street' because of its location, collapsed. The value of shares plunged to a fraction of their previous value. Shareholders were bankrupted.
- The crash was caused by many factors:
  1 Share prices rose too fast, and many people borrowed money to buy them. When the price started to go down, people panicked.
  2 Share prices did not reflect the true condition of the US economy.
  3 The US economy was in trouble before the crash; there was overproduction and unemployment was rising.
  4 The 'boom' had been financed by debt. This was all right while the economy expanded, but a disaster once people could not repay what they owed.
- The crash led to the Great Depression. Investment in industry slumped, unemployment increased, people had no money to spend. By 1932, 12 million people were out of work in the United States.
- The Depression spread to other countries, which led to a fall in international trade. Countries including the USA put higher tariffs (taxes) on imported goods in an attempt to protect jobs in their own industries. These tariffs just reduced trade still further.
- The government of President Hoover had little idea how to cope with the Depression. Like other Republicans, he believed in free enterprise, not in government interference in the economy.
- In the Presidential election of 1932, a Democrat, Franklin Roosevelt, was elected.

5 The United States of America, 1919–41

REVISION SUMMARY

4 THE NEW DEAL

- Roosevelt promised a 'New Deal' to the American people. By this he meant that his government would take whatever steps were necessary to deal with the Depression.
- In his first 'hundred days' in office, Roosevelt dealt with the most urgent problems, in particular by closing down all the weakest banks and providing emergency relief for the unemployed. During this period prohibition was repealed.
- The first New Deal (1933–5) aimed to solve America's unemployment crisis. A series of acts brought into being the 'Alphabetic Agencies', e.g.

  Civilian Conservation Corps (CCC)
  Works Progress Administration (WPA)
  Tennessee Valley Authority (TVA)
  National Recovery Administration (NRA)
  Home Owners Loan Corporation (HOLC).

  The Agricultural Adjustment Act helped farmers by forcing them to accept quotas which reduced overproduction. This helped prices recover.

- The second New Deal after 1935 dealt more with social issues, notably the Social Security Act (1935) which provided pensions and unemployment insurance.
- The New Deal had opponents, particularly among Republicans and rich businessmen who objected to government interference in private enterprise. The Supreme Court declared many of Roosevelt's plans illegal.
- Whether or not the New Deal was a success is difficult to say. Unemployment was reduced from a peak of nearly 13 million in 1933 to under 8 million in 1937, but it was only the Second World War which brought back full employment to the United States.

If you need to revise this subject more thoroughly, see the relevant topics in the Letts GCSE World History Study Guide.

The United States of America, 1919–41

QUESTIONS

1 Study Sources A, B, C, D and E, which relate to the stock market crash of 1929, and then answer questions (a)–(e) which follow.

SOURCE A

An extract from a popular song recorded by Bing Crosby in the early 1930s

Once I built a railway, I made it run,
Made it run against time.
Once I built a railway, now it's done.
Buddy, can you spare a dime?

Once I built a tower up to the sky,
Bricks and mortar and lime.
Once I built a tower, now it's done.
Buddy, can you spare a dime?

Gee, don't you remember – they called me 'Al',
It was 'Al' all the time.
Gee, don't you remember I'm your pal!
Buddy – can you spare a dime?

SOURCE B

A scene in New York, October 1929.

5 The United States of America, 1919–41

QUESTIONS

SOURCE C

A speech by President Hoover, 1928. Hoover was a Republican politician and a successful businessman.

We are faced with a peacetime choice between the American system of rugged individualism or state socialism. Socialist ideas would destroy the American way of life. It would have meant the undermining of the individual initiative and enterprise through which our people have grown to greatness. The Republican Party... restored the government to its position as an umpire instead of a player in the economic game.

SOURCE D

From a speech by F D Roosevelt, the Democrat candidate in the Presidential election of 1932

One of the duties of the state is that of caring for those of its citizens who find themselves the victims of such adverse circumstances as makes them unable to obtain even the necessities for mere existence.

SOURCE E

Automobiles and truck registrations, in millions

Year	Automobiles	Trucks
1920	8.1	1.1
1921	9.2	1.2
1922	10.7	1.5
1923	13.8	1.8
1924	15.4	2.1
1925	17.4	2.4
1926	19.2	2.8
1927	20.1	2.9
1928	21.3	3.1
1929	23.0	3.4
1930	22.0	3.5

(a) Study Sources A and B. What can you learn about the effects of the stock market crash of 1929 from these sources? (3)

(b) Study Source B. How reliable is this source as evidence of the effects of the stock market crash? Explain your answer fully. (4)

(c) Study Sources C and D.

  (i) In what ways do these sources show the differing attitudes of Hoover and Roosevelt about the 'duties of the state'. (3)

  (ii) Using the sources, and your own knowledge, how would you explain these differences? (5)

The United States of America, 1919–41

(d) Study all the sources. Do these sources provide enough evidence for you to say why there was a stock market crash in the USA in 1929? Explain your answer with reference to the sources. (5)

ULEAC 1993

2 Study Sources A–E which refer to the New Deal. Then answer **all** the questions.

SOURCE A

From an interview, published in 1970, with Blackie Gold, who had been unemployed during the Depression

I was in the CCC for six months. I came home for fifteen months, looked around for work and couldn't make $30 a month, so I enlisted back into the CCC and went to Michigan. I spent another 6 months there planting trees and building forests. And came out. But still no money to be made. So back into the CCC again and spent four and a half months fighting fires.

SOURCE B

A US newspaper cartoon entitled, 'The Spirit of the New Deal', published during Roosevelt's presidency. All three figures are wearing the badge of the National Industrial Recovery Administration.

SOURCE C

A notice displayed on the walls of 'Thomas Edison Inc.' of New Jersey, in April 1933, by the owner

President Roosevelt has done his part: now you do something. Buy something – buy anything, anywhere; paint your kitchen, give a party, get a car, pay a bill, rent a flat, get a haircut, see a show, build a house, take a trip, sing a song, get married. It does not matter what you do – but get going and keep going. The old world is starting to move.

5 The United States of America, 1919–41

QUESTIONS

SOURCE D

A graph showing the numbers of unemployed people (in millions) in the USA, 1929–42.

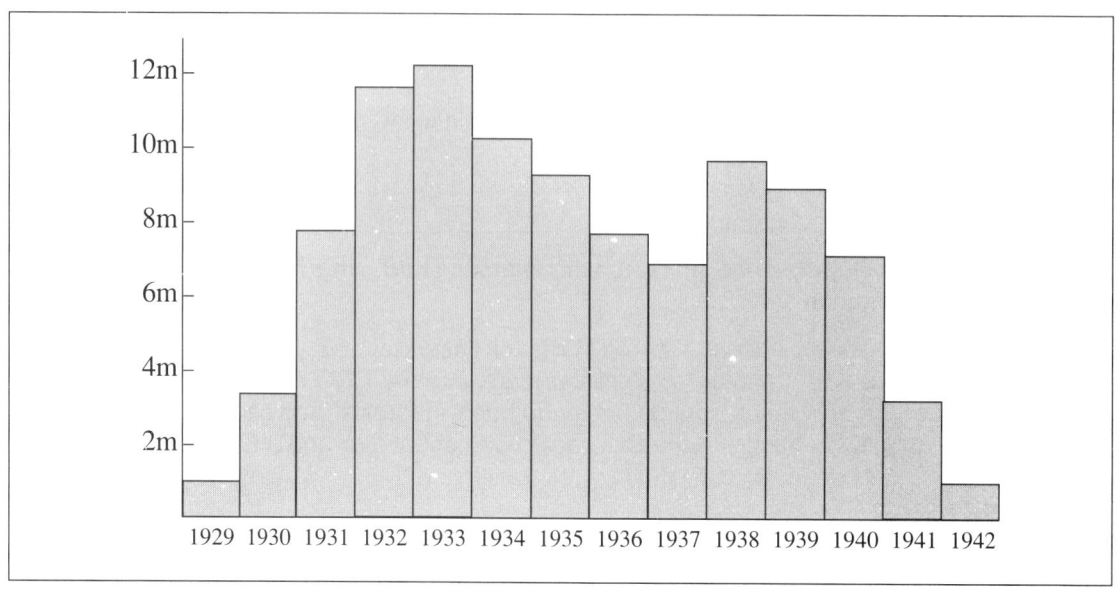

SOURCE E

Louis Banks recalls his life under the New Deal. He was interviewed in 1970.

I was so glad when war came and I got in the army. I knew I was safe. I put a uniform on, and I said, 'Now I am safe.' I had money coming, I had food coming, and I had a lot of friends round me. I knew that on the streets or hoboing, I might be killed any time.

(a) Study Source A. What is meant by the 'CCC'? (2)

(b) Study Source C. How would the instruction 'Buy something' help President Roosevelt's policies succeed? (2)

(c) Study Source D. In what ways would this graph be useful to an historian studying the New Deal? Explain your answer. (6)

(d) Study Source B and Source E. Which of these two views of the results of the New Deal is the more reliable? Explain your answer. (8)

(e) Study **all** the sources. 'The New Deal was not successful in restoring prosperity.' Do these sources show this view is true? Explain your answer fully. (12)

MEG 1993

Events in the 1930s leading to the Second World War 6

REVISION SUMMARY

1 INTRODUCTION
- Events in the 1930s saw the breakdown of the international security system established by the Treaty of Versailles. This was caused partly by the aggression of Italy, Germany and Japan, and partly by the failure of the League of Nations and the other major powers to stand up to them.

2 ITALY
- In 1922 the leader of the Fascist Party, Mussolini, became Prime Minister of Italy. He was soon dictator. He had dreams of building a great new Italian empire to rival the old Roman empire.
- In 1935 Italy invaded and conquered Ethiopia. The League of Nations did little. In 1936 Mussolini and Hitler set up the Rome-Berlin Axis, agreeing to support each other. Later Japan joined the Axis.

3 GERMANY
- In 1933 Adolf Hitler became Chancellor of Germany. He was helped to power by the economic depression in Germany. He was also popular because he promised to undo many of the provisions of the Treaty of Versailles.
- Hitler wanted to rebuild the German armed forces. He promised to regain land taken from Germany by the Treaty of Versailles, especially those territories where many Germans still lived. He wanted *Anschluss* (union) with Austria and *Lebensraum* (living space) for Germany in the east of Europe.
- Many people in Britain and France believed that the Treaty of Versailles had been unfair to Germany and thought that Hitler's demands were reasonable, especially as he appeared to be a counterbalance to the communist Soviet Union. This led Britain and France into adopting a policy of appeasement towards Hitler. This policy has been criticized by some who claim it convinced Hitler he could get away with his aggressive policies. Others have seen it as a genuine attempt to maintain peace when neither France nor Britain were strong enough to fight. It gave them time to rebuild their armed forces.
- In March 1936 the German army marched into the Rhineland. Neither Britain nor France did anything. Hitler promised that all he wanted now was peace.
- In March 1938 the German army marched into Austria. Austria became part of Germany (*Anschluss*).
- In September 1938 Hitler announced he was prepared to invade the Sudetenland region of Czechoslovakia in order to protect the Germans there. On 29 September, the Munich agreement was reached between Germany, Italy, Britain (represented by Neville Chamberlain) and France. The Sudetenland was given to Germany. Hitler promised that the rest of Czechoslovakia was safe. Chamberlain was sure he had prevented war and returned to Britain in triumph. In March 1939 German troops invaded the rest of Czechoslovakia. Britain and France did nothing.
- In August 1939 Hitler signed the Nazi-Soviet Pact with Stalin. They agreed to divide Poland between them. This left Hitler free to act in the west as he did not have to worry about an attack from the Soviet Union.
- On 1 September 1939 German troops invaded Poland. On 3 September Britain and France declared war on Germany.

If you need to revise this subject more thoroughly, see the relevant topics in the Letts GCSE World History Study Guide.

4 JAPAN
- Japan was hit hard by the world economic crisis of 1929–33. The country earned all its money by exporting goods, but nobody could afford to buy them. In 1931 Japan invaded Manchuria (part of China). Manchuria had raw materials and would provide a market for Japanese goods. The League of Nations was powerless to act.
- In 1936 Japan signed a pact with Germany. In 1937 Japan invaded the rest of China. In 1941 it invaded Indo-China. The USA replied by banning trade with Japan. In December 1941 the Japanese airforce attacked the American naval base at Pearl Harbor.

6 Events in the 1930s leading to the Second World War

QUESTIONS

1 Study the source below and then attempt **all** parts of this question.

Germany in 1936.

from a German atlas published in 1936

(a) Has this map any value for a study of German expansion in the years 1936–9? Explain your answer. (5)

(b) By October 1938 both Austria and the Sudetenland area of Czechoslovakia had become part of Germany. Did Germany use the same methods to gain control of these two areas? Explain your answer. (8)

(c) How did the attitudes of the British and French governments towards German actions change in 1939? (6)

(d) From the time that Hitler came to power in 1933, Germany and the Soviet Union fought a war of words. Yet in August 1939 the Soviet Union signed a pact with Germany. Why did the Soviet Union take this action? (6)

SEG 1992

The Cold War 7

REVISION SUMMARY

1 INTRODUCTION
- The 'Cold War' was the period of hostility between the Communist nations (led by the USSR) and the capitalist nations (led by the USA) which followed the Second World War.
- The Cold War never developed into fighting between the USSR and the USA. It was a struggle for influence in the world, created by the hatred which existed between the superpowers.
- The Cold War was at its peak while Stalin was alive. After his death in 1953, the Cold War continued, but as the years passed, tension between the superpowers slowly reduced.

2 THE END OF THE SECOND WORLD WAR
- While the Second World War lasted, the USA and the USSR worked together to defeat the common enemy, the Axis powers. Once the war stopped, hostility between the USSR and the western democracies was bound to surface again.
- As the war came to an end, the Allied leaders met to decide on arrangements for peacemaking, and in particular on the future of Germany and eastern Europe:
    1 At Yalta (February 1945), they agreed that, once defeated, Germany would be split into four zones of occupation. In eastern Europe free elections would be held to choose new governments in countries liberated from Germany. The United Nations Organization would be established as a replacement for the League of Nations.
    2 At Potsdam (July–August 1945), Poland's boundaries were agreed and arrangements for splitting Germany and Berlin into four zones were confirmed.
- However, between the two conferences much had changed. At Yalta, the USA was represented by President Roosevelt, who was prepared to cooperate with Stalin. The Potsdam Conference took place after Roosevelt's death, and his successor, President Truman, was more suspicious of Soviet motives.
- After Yalta, Stalin's determination to force a Communist government on Poland became clearer. Western fears of a Communist takeover in eastern Europe increased rapidly.
- Soviet suspicion of the USA increased after the atom bomb attacks on Japan. The USA had kept secret the development of this new weapon.
- By 1946 relations between the USSR and the West had deteriorated badly. Churchill, in a speech in the USA, referred to an 'Iron Curtain' which stretched across Europe 'from Stettin in the Baltic to Trieste in the Adriatic'.

3 THE COLD WAR IN EUROPE, 1946–55
- Between 1945 and 1948 most of eastern Europe fell under the control of Communist governments. These governments were all, with the exception of Yugoslavia led by Tito, under Stalin's control.
- Truman was determined to stop the spread of Communism. In 1947 the Truman Doctrine promised that the USA would support any nation threatened by Communist takeover. American and British intervention led to the Communists losing the civil war in Greece.
- In 1947 Truman took another step in fighting Communism by putting forward the Marshall Plan, which promised American aid to European countries to help them rebuild their war-damaged economies.
- The most serious crisis of the early years of the Cold War took place over Berlin in 1948–9. Disagreements over the administration of the zones of occupation came to a head when the western allies agreed to establish a single government in their zones and to introduce a new currency in order to help Germany's economic recovery. This was completely opposite to Stalin's policy, which was to keep Germany as weak as possible.

7 The Cold War

REVISION SUMMARY

- Berlin, although itself split into four zones, was completely surrounded by the Soviet zone of occupation. In June 1948 Stalin ordered that all land communications between West Berlin and the outside world should be cut off. The Berlin blockade lasted until May 1949 and West Berlin only survived because of the airlift of supplies organized by the western allies. Eventually Stalin gave way. As a result of the crisis, two new states, the German Federal Republic (West Germany) and the German Democratic Republic (East Germany) were set up in 1949.

- In 1949 the western democracies set up a new military alliance called NATO (North Atlantic Treaty Organization). In 1955 the Soviet Union set up its own alliance, the Warsaw Pact.

4 THE COLD WAR IN ASIA

- The establishment of the Communist regime in China in 1949 caused an extension of the Cold War.

- The outbreak of the Korean War in 1950 led to the intervention of the USA and other western powers, fighting on behalf of the United Nations, to resist aggression by Communist North Korea against the South. China then joined the war in support of the North. The fighting lasted for three years, at the end of which Korea remained divided.

- Chinese support also helped establish a Communist government in North Vietnam. In 1954 France, the colonial power in Indo-China, was defeated at Dien Bien Phu by the North Vietnamese. The Geneva Agreements of 1954 saw France withdraw from Indo-China. Vietnam was temporarily partitioned, and Laos and Cambodia established as independent states.

- The Geneva Agreements did not solve the problems of Vietnam. By the early 1960s the Americans were giving military help to the South Vietnamese government to prevent a Communist takeover. The fighting in South Vietnam rapidly developed into a full-scale war which continued until 1975 when the Communists took over and reunited the country. The USA had been forced to withdraw from Vietnam by 1973.

5 PEACEFUL COEXISTENCE AND THE CUBAN MISSILE CRISIS

- The process of deStalinization and the emergence of Khrushchev as the leader of the Soviet Union after 1956 led to a relaxation of tension in the Cold War. The USA did not intervene when the USSR crushed the Hungarian uprising in 1956, and periodic meetings between Soviet and western leaders took place.

- However, in 1960 arrangements for a summit meeting in Paris were thrown into chaos by the shooting down of an American U-2 spy plane over the Soviet Union. The Cold War, for a couple of years, broke out again.

- In 1961, in order to prevent people escaping into West Berlin, the Communist government of East Germany ordered a wall to be built dividing the city into its eastern and western zones. Many people subsequently died trying to cross the wall. The wall became a symbol of Communist tyranny in eastern Europe.

- In 1962 the most dangerous crisis of the Cold War occurred over Cuba. When the USA discovered that the Soviet Union was constructing missile bases in Cuba, it placed a naval blockade around the island to prevent the bases being completed. The world was threatened with a nuclear war between the superpowers. Eventually Khrushchev backed down and agreed to dismantle the bases.

- The Cuban missile crisis led directly to improved relations between the USA and the USSR. The 'hotline' – a direct telephone line on which the US and Soviet Presidents could talk to each other – was set up, and in 1964 the first major step in limiting nuclear weapons took place with the signing of the Test Ban Treaty.

- Although considerable suspicion between the USA and the USSR remained, relations between the two after 1962 were generally conducted on the basis of peaceful coexistence.

If you need to revise this subject more thoroughly, see the relevant topics in the Letts GCSE World History Study Guide.

The Cold War 7

1 Study Sources A, B, C, D and E, which relate to the Marshall Plan, and then answer questions (a) to (e) which follow.

SOURCE A

Extract from a speech by US Secretary of State, George Marshall, June 1947

Our policy is directed not against any country or doctrine but against hunger, poverty, desperation and chaos. Its purpose should be the revival of a working economy in the world.

SOURCE B

Andrei Vyshinsky, Soviet Foreign Minister, September 1947

As is now clear, the Marshall Plan is clearly just another version of the Truman Doctrine adapted to the conditions of postwar Europe. In bringing forward this plan, the United States government counted on the cooperation of the governments of the United Kingdom and France to limit the freedom of choice in Europe.

SOURCE C

A British historian, writing in 1984

The very day that Marshall's plan was proclaimed, Britain moved into action. Key Foreign Office personnel drew up, within the next two weeks, a programme that involved Britain itself taking the lead, perhaps using the European Economic Commission as a basis, to turn the Marshall Plan into a practical reality.

SOURCE D

The first Marshall Aid arrives in Europe, 1948.

7 The Cold War

QUESTIONS

SOURCE E

A map of Europe in 1948. The shaded areas show those countries which received aid from the United States. The total value of this aid was £22,400 billion.

(a) Study Source A. Explain in your own words why, according to this source, Marshall Aid was introduced. (3)

(b) Study Sources A and B. In what ways do these sources show differing attitudes towards the Marshall Plan? (3)

(c) Using Sources A and B, and your own knowledge, how would you explain the differences between these two sources? (5)

(d) Study Sources A, B and C. How useful are Sources A, B and C for understanding the purposes of the Marshall Plan? Explain your answer by reference to the sources. (4)

(e) Study Sources C, D and E. Do these sources provide you with enough evidence to explain how the Marshall Plan was put into operation in Europe? Explain your answer with reference to the sources. (5)

ULEAC 1993

2 During the Second World War the USA and the USSR fought on the same side. From 1945 to 1955 there were many serious disagreements between these two countries. The following questions ask you about this change in relations between the USA and the USSR.

(a) (i) Name the leader of the USSR who attended the Yalta Conference in 1945. (1)

The Cold War 7

QUESTIONS

(ii) Explain what is meant by the 'Truman Doctrine'. **Briefly** use your knowledge of the USA's policy towards Communism between 1945 and 1955 to support your answer.
(3)

(b) How **similar** were the following to each other:
   I   the Yalta Conference;
   II the Potsdam Conference? (6)

(c) Which **one** of the following was the most important reason why relations became very poor between the USA and the USSR by 1955:
   I   the 'Iron Curtain';
   II   the division of Germany;
   III Marshall Aid?

Explain your answer fully by referring to I, II and III. (15)

MEG 1994

Answers

1 THE FIRST WORLD WAR, 1914–18

Question	Answer	Mark
1 (a)	Study Source D. What was a 'Pals' Battalion?	2

Examiner's tip A straightforward question, and only a brief definition is required. But do avoid giving a general answer such as 'It was made up of groups of friends'. Much better is, 'It was a battalion formed by volunteers who worked in the same business or lived in the same area. They would all know each other.'

(b) Study Source E. What changes to the system of recruitment were made by the Military Services Bill of May 1916? 2

Examiner's tip As in question 1 avoid a general answer such as 'It introduced conscription'. This will get you 1 mark. To get the full 2 marks, you need to give a little more detail, as in the answer below.

This made it compulsory for all men, including married men, between the ages of 18 and 41 to join the army.

(c) Study Source C. In what ways might these figures be useful to an historian studying British recruitment in the First World War? Explain your answer. 6

Examiner's tip The key to this question is to use your knowledge of the topic to make full use of Source C. If you fail to do this, then all you will be able to do is to explain that the list is useful for showing that recruiting figures went up and down, with an overall decline. This will not get you many marks. However, using your wider knowledge of the topic, you can explain how the changes in the figures reflect military disasters such as Gallipoli, changes in public opinion and recruiting campaigns. The following answer would achieve full marks. Again the key is to base your answer on precise knowledge, rather than on generalizations.

The figures would be useful because they show what public opinion was like during the war. In August and September 1914 hundreds of thousands joined up because they thought they would be home by Christmas. A lot of pressure was put on them to make them join the army: propaganda posters, women pinned white feathers on men out of uniform, and music halls sang patriotic songs to persuade men to join. The war can be traced through the figures, as news came of the atrocious conditions men were less keen to join up. There is a big drop in October 1914 after the Battle of the Marne made it clear the war would not be over quickly, and in December 1915 with the failure of the Gallipoli campaign the figures go right down again. So the figures show how the public reacted to the events in the war.

(d) Study Sources A and B. Which of these two sources gives the more reliable view of British attitudes to recruitment? Explain your answer. 8

Answers to Unit 1

Question	Answer	Mark

Examiner's tip — The reliability of these two sources as evidence of attitudes towards recruitment can be judged by crossreferencing to the other sources, to your knowledge of the topic and by considering the purpose of Source A. Do not base your answer on statements such as 'Diaries are unbiased and can be trusted', 'He was a clergyman so he can be trusted', 'Posters cannot be trusted'. The following answer uses crossreferencing and background knowledge well, and would get full marks.

Source A is a recruiting poster to encourage men to join the army. It is reliable as evidence of how propaganda was used in recruitment as it is typical of the posters seen all over Britain. Such posters were a central part of the government's campaign as can be seen in Source B where the men are annoyed with all the posters. Sources C and D show that posters like this were effective as men did at first join up in great numbers, so they were enthusiastic towards recruitment. The words the poster uses also show that most people regarded it as cowardly not to join up. It plays on men's guilt and what their families will think of them. Most people must have agreed with this view otherwise the poster would not have worked. But Sources C and E also show that not everyone was persuaded to join up. This was why conscription was needed in 1916. Source B shows the views of farmers. They want men left to work on the farms. But they do not object to conscription because this would be fair to everyone. They only represent the views of a few farmers but we do know from Sources C and E that other people must have felt the same about volunteering. We also know that some people did not agree with conscription because they became conscientious objectors. So both sources give us some reliable evidence but there are ways in which both are not reliable.

(e) Study all the sources. 'Conscription was introduced because voluntary recruitment was not working.' Do these sources provide reliable evidence to show this view to be true? Explain your answer carefully. | 12

Examiner's tip — You must not describe each source one after the other. You are expected to judge whether the sources as a collection provide reliable evidence for the statement. Make sure you use all of the sources and crossreference between them. Do not claim that the photograph is a fake; the caption tells you it is genuine. The answer below would score full marks. It evaluates each source carefully and crossreferences between them well.

The very fact that Source A had to be issued might reflect unwillingness on the part of some men to volunteer although 1914 is a bit early to make this judgement. It probably means the government expected volunteering to be unpopular with some men so they would need persuading. Source B seems to confirm these fears, the farmers did not want to volunteer. But it also shows that the posters were not working. Of course Source B is only about a few farmers whereas Source C shows national trends. This does show a big fall off in numbers of men volunteering, only 55,000 in December 1915. This

Answers to Unit 1

Question	Answer	Mark

supports Source B and shows that voluntary recruitment was no longer sufficient and that conscription was needed. Source D appears to show voluntary recruitment working but it could have been chosen as propaganda to show success. It does not mean that people were volunteering like this all over the country. Source E has to be read carefully. The King claims that voluntary recruitment has been a success. Why then is he introducing conscription? This shows the opposite to what he is claiming and is supported by the figures in Source C. So, overall these sources do show that voluntary recruitment was not working.

---

2 (a) **The poster points out the danger to Britain of German submarines. German submarines sank many ships carrying supplies to Britain. Was this the most serious way in which British civilians were affected by enemy action? Explain your answer.**   **10**

> **Examiner's tip** This question is asking for a judgement about what was the most serious way in which civilians were affected by enemy action. The poster shows you one way: food supplies from America being disrupted by German U-boats. You need to explain the effects of this in more detail, then describe other ways in which civilians were affected by enemy action. Finally, you should reach a judgement about which had the most serious effect. Other ways in which civilians were affected by enemy action could include attacks by the German navy on coastal towns, bombing by aircraft and Zeppelin airships, families losing loved ones in action on the western front. The answer below explains the effects of several of these and comes to a sensible judgement.

The First World War was the first time civilians were affected badly by enemy action. Although cities were bombed, the main way most people were affected was by food and fuel supplies being cut off.

The campaign by German submarines to cut off Britain's supplies was serious. Britain was not selfsufficient and had to import large amounts of food. When the war started there had been panic buying but then things settled down and food shortages did not become serious until 1917 when Germany declared unrestricted submarine warfare on ships going to Britain. Large numbers of ships were sunk and food shortages became serious. Prices went up and there were food queues everywhere. There were shortages of butter and meat and even bread. Fuel was also short. Coal was rationed and many people had no way of warming their houses or of cooking. The situation got so bad that in 1918 the government had to introduce food rationing. This helped a bit with everyone getting some meat, bacon and butter every week.

Some people were affected by attacks by the German navy. In 1914 Scarborough and other towns on the east coast were attacked and people were killed, but it was not repeated. More people were killed by Zeppelin airships. These bombed big cities like London from 1914 to 1916 and then planes took over. But although people were killed it was nothing like in the Second World War where hundreds of thousands of people had to be evacuated.

Answers to Unit 1

Question	Answer	Mark

The bombing did continue throughout the years whereas food shortages only got serious from 1917, but the food shortages affected far more people, some of whom were close to starving.

(b) **The poster above is an example of propaganda. Propaganda was very widely used during the First World War. Why was this the case?**   **10**

> **Examiner's tip** For this question you need to explain several reasons why propaganda was widely used. These reasons could include: to persuade men to join the army and to make sure the civilian population was fully behind the war effort. You need to explain that civilians were crucial to the war effort in ways never known before so the government had to win their support. You should give a concise explanation of why propaganda was used with these two groups.

The First World War needed millions of men to do the fighting. Both sides hoped to win simply by having more men than the other side. There were few machines to do the fighting. Until 1916 the British government relied on volunteers for the army. These men had to be persuaded to join up through propaganda. They had to be made to hate the Germans, or to feel ashamed if they did not join up. Pressure was also put on wives and girlfriends to persuade their men to join up. After 1916, this propaganda was not so important because of conscription.

In Britain large amounts of armaments had to be produced for the war effort, food had to be produced by fewer workers, people had to work in unpleasant and dirty jobs they were not used to, and many had to put up with shortages of food and fuel. These efforts of civilians were crucial otherwise the army would have had no weapons and the war effort would have collapsed.

The morale of the civilians had to be kept up especially as the war dragged on. If it collapsed, and support for the war went, the war would have been lost. The government used propaganda to achieve all this. It tried to make people first hate the Germans, and then appealed to their patriotism. Propaganda was also important to hide from people how terrible it really was in the trenches. If they had known this they might not have supported the war so the truth had to be kept from them.

Propaganda was vital to keep the war going.

(c) **The poster has a woman as its central character. In what ways did women become increasingly important to the war effort?**   **10**

> **Examiner's tip** This question requires you to explain the role women played in helping the war effort. The word 'increasingly' is important, as it suggests that you have to show how their contribution became more important as the war went on. What follows is the basis for a good answer. Expansion of the points mentioned would be needed to gain full marks.

Women did not take over many men's jobs until 1915, when there was a serious shortage of armaments. Women worked in munitions factories.

Answers to Unit 2

Question	Answer	Mark

But the real change did not come until 1916 and conscription. This led to a massive shortage of labour and women began to work in all types of factories, and as mechanics, bus drivers and in government offices. Women also performed an important role by producing food on the farms through the Women's Land Army.

2 THE PEACE TREATIES OF 1919–20 AND THE LEAGUE OF NATIONS

Question	Answer	Mark

1 (a) (i) Name the treaty that was signed between the Allies and Austria in 1919. — **1**

> **Examiner's tip** — The Treaty of St Germain is the full answer, but St Germain or even Germain would also be enough to gain the mark. Some students who can remember the names of the treaties at the end of the war, but cannot recall which treaty was made with each country, write out a list of **all** the treaties and hope that the Examiner will allow it on the basis that the list includes the correct one. Unfortunately, this does not work.

(ii) Explain what is meant by the phrase 'dictated settlement'. Briefly use your knowledge of the Treaty of Versailles to support your answer. — **3**

> **Examiner's tip** — You are asked to define an historical term, but also to place it in the context of the Treaty of Versailles. Take notice of the word **briefly**. This indicates that a lengthy, detailed answer is not needed to earn the marks; if you ignore this instruction you will just be wasting valuable time. The following answer gives a precise definition, and then links it to the Treaty of Versailles, which is all that is needed for the three marks.

A dictated settlement is a treaty ending a war in which one side decides on the terms of the treaty and forces the other side to accept these terms, whether it likes it or not. There is no negotiation between the two sides. This is what happened with the Treaty of Versailles. The Germans were presented with the peace terms, and had no choice but to sign. They were not consulted about the terms of the treaty. In fact, their name for the treaty was the 'Diktat'.

(b) How different from each other were the following:
I   The Treaty of Sèvres, 1920;
II The Treaty of Lausanne, 1923? — **6**

> **Examiner's tip** — Questions which ask 'How similar...?' or 'How different...?' cannot be answered properly by considering **only** similarity **or** difference. When judging how different these two treaties were, don't forget that the extent of the similarities between them is also important. If there were many similarities, then the treaties cannot be very different. The best answers to this question will, then, identify differences, but will also deal with similarities before reaching a conclusion. Given that there are only six marks at stake, you would not be expected to include any more than three or four similarities and differences.

Answers to Unit 2

Question	Answer	Mark

These were both treaties made between Turkey and the Allies (**similarity**), but Sèvres was rejected by the Turks whereas Lausanne was accepted by them (**difference**). The main reason for this was that most Turks thought that the terms of Sèvres were far too harsh, but Lausanne was much more fair towards them (**difference**). At Lausanne they regained control of the Straits, whereas at Sèvres the Straits had been put under international control, and they also regained Eastern Thrace from Greece which had been taken away at Sèvres (**differences**). However, some of the terms were the same, the treatment of the Arab parts of the Ottoman Empire for instance, where some areas gained independence and others became mandates (**similarity**). Overall, then, Lausanne was different enough from Sèvres for the Turks to accept it.

(c) 'The following two leaders were very pleased with the terms of the Treaty of Versailles:

I Prime Minister Clemenceau of France;
II President Wilson of the USA.'

Do you agree with this statement? Explain your answer fully by referring to I, II and the terms of the Treaty of Versailles. 15

> **Examiner's tip**
>
> This question is concerned with the links between the terms of the Treaty of Versailles, and the attitudes of the peacemakers, in this case Clemenceau and Wilson. You need to know what the peacemakers *wanted*, and *whether or not they achieved it*. In fact what happened was that each of the peacemakers achieved *some* of their aims, but not others. So, in tackling this question, you need to look at four separate issues, in relation to the terms of the Treaty:
>
> - What did Wilson achieve – how *pleased* was he?
> - What did Wilson not achieve – how *displeased* was he?
> - What did Clemenceau achieve – how *pleased* was he?
> - What did Clemenceau not achieve – how *displeased* was he?
>
> By analysing these four issues you will be able to reach the balanced conclusion about the consequences of the Treaty that the question requires.

Nobody got everything they wanted out of the Treaty of Versailles because, to some extent, the Allies wanted different things. Wilson said he wanted a just and fair peace based on his 14 points. He got the most important point which was the creation of the League of Nations, and he believed that the League would deal with any problems that the Treaty left unsolved. So although he was less keen than the other Allies on punishing Germany, he was prepared to accept the final Treaty.

However, Wilson was disillusioned by the extent to which his original plans had to be abandoned. Self-determination was one of his ideas, but there were many examples in the treaties of this being ignored. In the Versailles Treaty many German areas such as Danzig and the Saar were taken away from Germany. Wilson had hoped to build a new fairer and safer world in the Treaty, but it was obvious that he had not been able to do this.

Clemenceau was determined that Germany would be punished and

Answers to Unit 2

Question	Answer	Mark

made so weak that France would never again be threatened by German power. On the face of it he got much of what he wanted. Germany's armed forces were strictly limited, she lost a lot of territory, she had to pay reparations, and she had to accept blame for the war.

However, the other Allies were suspicious of France's motives and were not prepared to give in to Clemenceau's more extreme demands. France was not allowed, for instance, to annex the Rhineland, which would have given her a much more defensible frontier with Germany.

So although both Wilson and Clemenceau were probably fairly pleased by the terms of the Treaty, it would be a mistake to say that they were very pleased because both of them failed to gain exactly what they wanted.

---

2 (a) Name the city where the League of Nations had its headquarters. 1

Geneva.

(b) Study Source A. How useful is this source for an historian writing about the setting up of the League of Nations? Use the source and your own knowledge to give reasons for your answer. 7

> **Examiner's tip** In judging how useful a source is there are several questions to consider. What does it tell me? Can I believe what it tells me? What does it not tell me? What do I want to find out? Source A gives some factual information about the first session of the Assembly of the League of Nations. We can say it is useful in giving us this information. There is no reason to doubt the reliability of this source, since our knowledge of the topic tells us that the USA did not become a member of the League, and that Germany, Austria, Bulgaria, Turkey and Russia were not members in 1920. But the source is of a straightforward, factual nature. It does not contain anything unusual, unknown, controversial or debatable, so we are likely to conclude that its usefulness is limited.
>
> The question tells you to judge the utility of the source for an historian writing about the setting up of the League, so your answer should focus on this issue, using your knowledge of the topic, as in the following example.

Source A gives us information about the first session of the Assembly of the League. It tells us that the United States was not represented, and that other countries, including Germany, were not members of the League. These facts are true, and so the source is reliable, and therefore useful, for the factual information it gives. However, it does not tell us anything much more than some basic facts, and there are many aspects of the setting up of the League that this source does not touch upon at all. Why was the League set up? Why did the USA not become a member? Why were some nations not included in the membership? A historian looking into the setting up of the League would need to explore issues like the treatment of the defeated powers, and the United States' rejection of the League, and this source does not help to do this. Its usefulness is therefore very limited.

Answers to Unit 2

Question	Answer	Mark
(c)	**Do Sources B and C explain fully why the League of Nations failed to achieve disarmament? Use the sources and your own knowledge to give reasons for your answer.**	7

Examiner's tip

Here the task is to decide whether Sources B and C give **enough** evidence to explain why the League did not achieve disarmament; the words to notice in the question are 'explain **fully**'. The first step, then, is to judge whether the sources give **any** evidence of the League's failure, as only after we have done that can we judge whether the evidence is sufficient or not.

Source B is an extract from the League's Covenant which states the aim of reducing armaments as far as possible. It says nothing of the League's failure to achieve this. Source C is the view of a British politician writing in 1932, by which time the Disarmament Conference was meeting, but not making much progress. The reliability of this source is an issue; we do not know who the politician was, or whether, for instance, he was involved in the Conference or not. However, it is possible to make some judgement of reliability on the basis of how accurately the source reflects the situation at that time as we know it. The source suggests that one of the reasons for the failure of nations to agree to disarmament was their distrust of each other, which is obviously true, so the source does provide **some** relevant evidence on the reasons for the League's failure. What it obviously cannot do is explain **fully** why the League failed to achieve disarmament, which is what the question asked. There were other factors not mentioned, or not fully explained, in the sources, and your answer should indicate what these were. The following example does this well.

> Sources B and C on their own cannot show why the League failed to achieve disarmament, although they can suggest some reasons for the League's failure. Source B says armaments should be reduced to the lowest point consistent with national safety, but nations could never agree about when they felt safe or not. As Source C shows, by the time they got to the Disarmament Conference in 1932 the level of distrust between nations was very high, and in that atmosphere nobody was going to agree to disarmament. The League had no means of forcing people to accept disarmament if they did not want it, and even during the 1920s there had been examples of where the League had been unsuccessful in dealing with aggression, such as the Corfu Incident. So in the more violent atmosphere of the 1930s, after the Japanese invasion of Manchuria, it was not a good time to get people to agree on disarmament. Source C shows that nations were becoming even more concerned about issues of security; Germany's government was in a state of chaos which would soon lead to Hitler coming to power, so the French wanted more security not less. Russia was not a member of the League, and would not be bound by any agreements on disarmament in the League. Other countries feared Russia, so they would not want to disarm. Sources B and C do not fully explain all these different reasons for the League's failure to achieve disarmament.

(d)	**An aim of the League of Nations was 'to encourage international cooperation'. Use Source D and your own knowledge to show how the League was organized to try to achieve this aim.**	9

Answers to Unit 2

Question	Answer	Mark

Examiner's tip Source D lists several organizations within the League. The question requires you to look at the function of each of these organizations and to judge how far it contributed to international cooperation within the overall structure of the League, as in this example.

The League was based at Geneva and had a permanent civil service called the Secretariat. All member states were members of the **Assembly**. This met once a year, and held debates on any matters of international importance. Every state had equal voting rights, which made the Assembly like the Parliament of the League. It could pass resolutions, and it had control over the League's budget, but its power was limited because all decisions had to be unanimous. However, it was very significant as a forum in which nations could meet and attempt to solve problems through discussion rather than force.

The **Council** was in some ways more important than the Assembly. It had a smaller membership, consisting of the permanent members (Britain, France, Italy and Japan), and a variable number of members elected by the Assembly. It was intended to deal with international crises as they arose, and this is why the Great Powers tried to dominate it. However, as in the Assembly, decisions had to be unanimous, so it proved quite difficult for the Council to reach agreement. It also had no means of forcing nations to accept its decisions, which severely limited its authority.

The **Permanent Court of Justice** (Court of International Justice) was based in The Hague. The judges came from 15 different countries, and dealt with legal disputes between member states. However, its power was limited by the fact that it could only hear cases where both sides agreed in advance to accept the Court's decision. In practice, most serious disputes were never referred to the Court.

The League had many Commissions or Committees which were responsible for specific issues. One of the most important of these was the **Mandates' Commission**. This Commission was supposed to supervise the way in which all the Mandates awarded to countries in the peace treaties of 1919–20 were administered. Another was the **International Labour Organization** which tried to improve working conditions of people throughout the world.

By looking at all these organizations we can see that the League did do a lot to bring about international cooperation. In each of the bodies mentioned above countries worked together to try and solve international problems, and to make the world a safer and better place.

(e) **What does the cartoon in Source E tell an historian about the problems of the membership of the League of Nations? Use your own knowledge to support your answer.**   6

Answers to Unit 3

Question	Answer	Mark

Examiner's tip — This question requires you to interpret Source E, which shows John Bull (who represents Britain) pushing a loaded cart uphill. The cart is the League of Nations and it is loaded with sacks, each of which represents a member state. Two sacks, Germany and Japan, have dropped off the cart, and one more, Italy, looks as if it might drop off at any moment.

Pushing the cart is hard work, but John Bull is prepared to keep going, even though it is 'only half a league' – this has a double meaning: 'half a league' could mean the distance he has still to travel, but obviously the cartoonist is referring to the fact that not all countries were members of the League of Nations. Japan and Germany both left the League in 1933; Japan over the League's condemnation of its invasion of Manchuria, and Germany over rearmament.

By July 1935, when this cartoon was drawn, it was clear that Italy was likely to invade Abyssinia, which would cause another crisis for the League, and explains why the sack representing Italy is poised to fall off the cart. The cartoon is thus full of references to the difficulties faced by the League in maintaining its membership in the face of increasing international tension during the 1930s.

The following excellent answer does not simply **describe** what the cartoon shows; it also uses knowledge to **explain** the features of the cartoon, with reference to problems of membership of the League.

> Source E shows how difficult it was becoming by the mid 1930s to keep the membership of the League together. Britain is pushing the cart, which represents the League, but already some of the nations have dropped off the cart. Japan and Germany are lying on the ground, showing that they are no longer members. Japan left the League because of the invasion of Manchuria; when the League condemned their action, they left it. Once Hitler came to power in Germany he was just looking for a chance to leave the League, and disputes over disarmament gave him his excuse. It was obvious that the League was too weak to stand up to aggression. By 1935 Italy's plans to invade Abyssinia were becoming clear, which explains why Italy is shown as just about falling off the cart. So no matter how hard Britain (shown by John Bull) tries to keep the League together, it is just falling apart, which is what the cartoon shows.

3 GERMANY, 1919–39

Question	Answer	Mark
1 (a)	Study Source A. Give the name of:	
(i)	'Germany's most important coalmining and industrial area';	1
(ii)	the country which acted with France in this invasion.	1

Examiner's tip — Two straightforward questions, each carrying just 1 mark, so no more than the correct name is required. The answers are (i) the Ruhr and (ii) Belgium.

Answers to Unit 3

Question	Answer	Mark
(b)	**Study Source C. Give two reasons why Germany's middle classes were affected by the hyperinflation of 1923.**	2

> **Examiner's tip**
> It is important to note that this question is about the middle classes and not about Germans in general. For example, any answers which give reasons that apply to the working classes but not to the middle classes will not be given any marks. The important point is that the middle classes often relied on fixed incomes while prices were going up rapidly. Many depended on their income from professional fees, pensions, savings, rents, investments. The question is marked by awarding a mark for each correct reason, so any two of these would get 2 marks. No explanation is asked for, and you will only be wasting time if you write one, because no more marks are available for this question.

(c)	**Study Source B. In what ways might this source be useful to an historian studying Weimar Germany? Explain your answer.**	6

> **Examiner's tip**
> It is important to note that these figures relate to the inflation between 1918 and 1923, so do not make the mistake of confusing them with the later economic crisis after the Wall Street Crash in 1929.
>
> This question is asking you to make a judgement about the usefulness of Source B. Look first at what the source tells you. It shows rapid inflation from the end of the war to 1923 and it appears to be getting worse all the time. But the figures for 1923 show an incredible increase in prices, out of all proportion with what had been seen in the previous few years. We can then move on to making inferences from the source. It would be reasonable to infer that the inflation shown here would make life very difficult for most people. Their wages would buy less, but at least these could be increased. The middle classes on fixed incomes would be the hardest hit. You can use your knowledge of the period or the evidence in Sources C, D and E to develop this a little.
>
> You should also use your background knowledge and the other sources to explain the significance of the dates in the table. The inflation shown after 1918 is obviously connected with the ending of the war, the reparations Germany had to pay and the loss of its important iron ore and coalfields. Germany simply could not afford to pay the reparations and tried to make ends meet by issuing more and more paper money. This led to the inflation shown in the figures.
>
> The enormous rise in inflation in 1923 can be linked to the occupation of the Ruhr in 1923 by France and Belgium and the following further loss of industrial production (you could refer to what Source A tells you for this).
>
> So a good answer will state that the source shows us how bad inflation was and that it tells us when inflation worsened. We can infer from the figures how badly people would have suffered and who would most be affected. We can also work out, by relating the dates in Source B to our knowledge of events, or to the events described in Source A, something about the causes of this inflation.
>
> You will see that the following answer contains some of these ingredients, but by no means all of them. Think how you could improve this answer.

Source B shows the effect on prices that the German government policy of printing paper money in large amounts had. The source shows that because of this inflation the savings of the middle classes would soon be reduced to nothing as more and more money was required to buy basic food. Source B shows how the intensity of the hyperinflation increased as the occupation of the Ruhr went on. The last two columns show the increase in late 1923 getting much worse.

Answers to Unit 3

Question	Answer	Mark
(d)	**Study Source D and Source E. Which of these two sources gives the more reliable account of the effects of hyperinflation in Germany in 1923? Explain your answer.**	8

Examiner's tip This question requires you to use your knowledge of the period and/or the other sources to test the reliability of Sources D and E.

Do not make judgements based merely on the type of each source. For example, few marks would be awarded for any of these points:

- eye-witness accounts, so should be reliable
- written long after the event, so would have forgotten what really happened
- just one person's experiences, so does not prove anything.

Use your knowledge of the period to test what these sources tell us (you can see an example of this in the answer below where it refers to the boys making kites out of paper money). Use the other sources to test Sources D and E. There is plenty of scope for this in the question as the answer below also shows. This answer is a good one, but it does use the other sources better than it uses background knowledge, which is really only used once.

Note that you do not have to decide finally that one source is more reliable than the other. You can decide they are both reliable. What matters are the reasons you give for your answer.

Source D is an account of the effects of inflation from a middleclass housewife. It says that although her husband was an eye surgeon they lived virtually without any income, while businessmen were well off. It really only shows what happened to one family and she may be looking back and exaggerating but her account is supported by other sources. Source B shows the rapid rise in prices which would make her fixed income quickly worthless. You can see that by August 1923 her income would only buy a few eggs. They would also be badly off because her husband's patients were paying their fees three months late when the money would be worth a lot less because of the rapid inflation shown in Source B. So I think that the other sources show Source D to be reliable about the effects of inflation.

Source E says that salaries never kept up with inflation and the paper money became worthless. I know this is right because I have seen pictures of boys making kites out of bank notes because they were not worth anything so the story about the thieves leaving the money is probably true. The point Source E makes about people on fixed incomes is supported by Sources B and D which show that the middle classes whose income did not go up would be in trouble. So both sources are reliable because they are supported by other sources.

(e)	**Study all the sources. 'The economic crisis of 1923 brought equal suffering to all sections of the German people.' Do these sources provide reliable evidence to show this view to be true? Explain your answer carefully.**	12

Answers to Unit 3

| Question | Answer | Mark |

Examiner's tip Here you are being asked to test the sources for reliability to see if they can be used to support the statement about the 1923 crisis. Make sure you do not just use the sources at face value, that is just checking whether what they say agrees with the statement. You could have a source which agreed that the crisis did bring equal suffering, but it would not provide reliable evidence to show this view to be true if the source itself was unreliable.

In evaluating the sources you must read what they say, then check this against the other sources and against what you know about the period. The more sources you evaluate in this way the more marks you will get.

The sources appear to provide evidence that not all sections of the German people suffered equally. The middle classes are mentioned several times as suffering particularly badly because they were on fixed incomes; businessmen, such as factory owners, are mentioned as being better off; but workers in factories suffered because their wages did not keep up with inflation. You now have to decide if this is reliable evidence.

The following answer uses both knowledge of the period and crossreferencing between the sources to evaluate what the sources say. It also ends with a clear conclusion.

Sources A and B just give the factual background. They show that the situation in Germany was generally bad and that everyone would be affected. Germany had to import coal so this would be expensive, the government was printing money so people's wages and savings would be worth less than before, and prices were going up fast. So everybody would be hit. These sources do not, by themselves, tell us whether some people would be affected more than others.

When we add the evidence from the other sources we can see that some people were affected more badly. Sources C, D and E all show that the middle classes suffered worse than anyone else. Their fixed incomes did not go up at all while prices went up all the time, and sometimes they had to wait a long time for their money (Source D). They had to sell tin cans (Source C) to raise money. These sources support each other that the middle classes suffered the most. I know this is right. Many of the middle classes depended on their savings and these were wiped out by the inflation. It was many of the middle classes who began to support the Nazi party at this time because they were so badly off.

Source C is not reliable by itself. It only shows a few of the middle classes and could be unrepresentative, but Source D supports it and makes it more likely to be reliable. What Source D says is right, people with fixed incomes and people who depended on fees from others were in trouble. What she says about having a baby is a small personal story but does reflect the facts. Widows and pensioners would also be badly hit.

Source E supports all this about the middle classes. It also shows that everybody suffered. Workers had to take wheelbarrows to work to carry the money home in. But at least their wages could go up a bit, when the money for the middle classes did not go up at all. The people who would be better off would be big businessmen because they had a lot of money to protect them and farmers who could at least feed

Answers to Unit 3

Question	Answer	Mark

themselves from their own crops. These sources tell us little about these groups. There is a bit in Source D but nothing about the fact that some industrialists and landowners actually made big profits out of the crisis.

So these sources do show that everybody suffered, but not that they all suffered equally. They show the middle classes suffered the most. But they do not tell us anything about some groups in society.

---

2 (a) (i) Write a sentence explaining what National Socialists meant by the word 'Aryan'.   **2**

> **Examiner's tip** Make sure you write no more than a brief sentence. Get the main points down, e.g. the National Socialists believed that some races were superior to others, the most pure being the Aryan race to which Germans belonged; a typical Aryan was tall, longlegged, slim, with blond hair; to keep the purity of the race Aryans should not marry other races, which they considered to be inferior, such as the Jews (you would not need all these for 2 marks).

(ii) Write a sentence explaining what is meant by anti-semitism.   **2**

> **Examiner's tip** The following definition would be acceptable for 2 marks: 'Anti-semitism is racial prejudice against Jews as a distinct and inferior (barely human) race; in Germany it meant making Jews scapegoats for all Germany's problems and ended in violent persecution of Jews.'

(iii) Write one or two sentences explaining why there was so much anti-semitism in Germany during the 1930s.   **3**

> **Examiner's tip** This question requires a slightly longer answer. Some of the following reasons could be mentioned: Hitler's hatred of Jews, anti-Jewish laws that were passed, anti-Jewish propaganda, the indoctrination of young people, the encouragement of anti-semitism by the SA and SS, the distrust of Jews over the Treaty of Versailles and the economic crises of the 1920s. You would not be required to cover all of these reasons. Two or three would be enough, with a brief explanation. It is important that you do not just, for example, describe the laws, but that you briefly indicate how they encouraged anti-semitism.
>
> There are only 3 marks and you have to remember you have not got time, nor should you try, to write everything you know about the topic. You should not write anything longer than the answer below, and answers shorter than this could still score 3 marks if they are to the point.

There was so much anti-semitism because Hitler hated the Jews and he encouraged everyone else to do the same by using propaganda and making them believe that the Jews were the Germans' greatest enemy. The Nazis encouraged people to hate the Jews by taking part in things like Crystal Night when Jewish shops were smashed up. There was already a lot of feeling against the Jews because some Jewish businessmen had made lots of money in the 1920s and people thought they were bleeding Germany of its wealth.

Answers to Unit 3

Question	Answer	Mark

(iv) Write one or two sentences explaining why German Jews found it difficult to combat anti-semitism. — **3**

Examiner's tip Be careful not to repeat the points you made in the answer to (iii). Concentrate on the weak position the Jews were in against the might of the state. The following concisely gives a number of reasons.

> German Jews found it difficult to combat anti-semitism because of the support it got from the government. People were afraid to be friendly with Jews, they might get beaten up by the SA or SS who stopped them from shopping at Jewish shops. The Nazis were in control and it was difficult to fight it, even in schools children were taught to hate Jews. The Jews had different religious beliefs and often lived differently from everybody else so they were easy targets, how could they defend themselves?

(v) Write a paragraph describing the measures that were taken against Jews in Germany during the years 1933–9. — **5**

Examiner's tip Do not get carried away and write too much. You cannot score more than 5 marks no matter how much you write! Make sure you describe several measures briefly. This is better than writing a lot about one measure, or just writing a general account without identifying any actual measures.
An answer of nine to ten lines describing three or four of the measures detailed below would be sufficient to score full marks.

> Boycotting of Jewish shops and doctors.
> Nuremberg Laws of 1935 forbidding Jews German citizenship and making it illegal for them to marry Germans.
> Confiscation of Jewish property, 1938.
> Letter J stamped on Jewish passports.
> Crystal Night.

(b) How successful were the domestic policies of the German government in the years 1933–9? — **15**

Examiner's tip This question is rather different from the others. Not only does it require an essay answer, but it also asks you to make a judgement. This judgement must be based on accurate factual knowledge of the topic.
It is important that you cover a range of domestic policies of the Nazi government during this period, for example on young people, women, keeping control, the Jews, the churches, the economy and unemployment and dealing with opponents. You will not be expected to cover all of these areas, but at least four or five of them should be dealt with. For each policy you will need to reach a judgement about how successful the government was (to do this you need to consider what the government was trying to achieve). Remember that in some areas the extent of government success may have changed over time. Finally, an answer which deals with only one aspect of government policy, no matter how detailed, will never get high marks. Nor will an answer which is disorganized and jumps from one area to another at random. So make sure your answer is organized. The easiest way to do this is to deal with one area after another (making a judgement on

Answers to Unit 4

Question	Answer	Mark

each policy as you cover it) and then reach an overall conclusion at the end. Do not just describe what the government did; you must be analytical.

The following answer takes a critical but balanced look at several areas of policy, explains successes and failures, and is well supported by factual knowledge.

> Hitler's policy towards young people had mixed success. He tried to indoctrinate them into his ideas. Boys were to be physically strong and future leaders, while girls had to be wives and mothers. Hitler had some success in impressing his thinking upon young minds but his educational policies did lead to a drop in standards in academic work.
>
> Many young people were reluctant to join the Hitler Youth and in 1937 membership had to be made compulsory. This shows he was not winning everyone over. There were even some opposition groups like the White Rose. This held secret meetings and printed antiNazi pamphlets. But many students were proNazi and readily took part in rallies and book burnings. We cannot measure the long term success of these policies because the Reich fell before the young had been through the whole system.
>
> Hitler wanted women to keep to Children, Church and Cooking. For producing lots of pure German children, they were rewarded with money and the 'Mother's Cross'. They were discouraged from going out to work. The birth rate did go up but mainly because of the rise in standard of living rather than because of government inducements. But the rate was still below what it was in the 1920s. Later when conscription was introduced and armaments were needed the women were needed at work again. The Nazis had to change their policy thus defeating their earlier aims.
>
> Hitler had more success with economic policy. Unemployment nearly disappeared. Men were put on public works programmes, the motorways were built this way. But unemployment really went down because of conscription and the making of armaments. Most people had a better standard of living and were happy with the regime. There was little opposition, the SA and SS saw to that. But few people became convinced Nazis so Hitler's success was uneven.

4 RUSSIA, 1917–41

Question	Answer	Mark
1 (a) (i)	**Write a sentence to explain what is meant by the word 'abdicated' as used in the passage.**	2

Examiner's tip This question is asking you to define a word in its historical context. Abdication is when a monarch (king, queen, emperor, etc.) chooses to give up the throne. You would certainly get a mark just for knowing this, but to be sure of the 2 marks you should illustrate the link between abdication and the situation in Russia in March 1917, as in the following example.

Answers to Unit 4

Question	Answer	Mark

In March 1917 Nicholas II decided to give up his throne because of the revolution breaking out in Petrograd; this is what abdicated means in the passage.

(ii) Write a sentence to explain the meaning of the word 'Duma'.   2

Examiner's tip Again, you are asked to define a historical term. The Duma was the Russian parliament or elected council at the time of the revolution. If you could add some historical detail to your definition, you would certainly achieve 2 marks, as in this example.

The Duma was the Russian parliament which Nicholas II allowed to meet after the Revolution of 1905.

(iii) Write one or two sentences to explain why people were demonstrating in Petrograd in March 1917.   3

Examiner's tip Here, in a simple way, you are being asked to start thinking about the **causes** of events. The question does not ask for a lot of detail – it tells you to limit your answer to one or two sentences, and there are only 3 marks available. In questions like this do not make the mistake of trying to write too much; it is best to concentrate your efforts on those questions which carry the most marks. Your answer here need only mention two or three causal factors (reasons) for why people were demonstrating.

People were demonstrating because they were fed up with the war and the hardships it brought. Russia was losing the war, the people were starving, and they blamed the Tsar.

(iv) Write a paragraph to explain why the revolution was described as 'leaderless'.   4

Examiner's tip This question asks you to explain a judgement about the **nature** of the March Revolution. In what sense was it leaderless? Judgements must always be supported by reference to the facts, but as this question only carries 4 marks, it is clear that you are not expected to analyse the issue in depth. The following answer shows relevant knowledge, but is particularly strong because it explores different possible aspects of the word 'leaderless'.

When you compare it to the November Revolution it was leaderless. In November people like Lenin and Trotsky planned to take power, and they did. There were no such leaders in March, events were much more unplanned. People were hungry and had lost faith in the Tsar, so they rioted or went on strike. However, this does not mean that there were no leaders at all. In the Soviets there were revolutionaries who helped to stir up trouble, and the Duma refused to obey the Tsar's order to stop meeting. In a way these people were leaders, they were important and they helped the revolution to succeed, they just weren't as obvious as in November. However, the passage uses the word leaderless to make the point that the revolution was a kind of outburst which just swept the Tsar away, and you can't really doubt this. Everyone just wanted to get rid of him because Russia was in such a mess.

Answers to Unit 4

Question	Answer	Mark
(v)	Write a paragraph to explain why many people at the time blamed Tsar Nicholas for Russia's problems.	4

Examiner's tip Here again you are dealing with causal factors. Weaker answers will presume that describing Russia's problems – particularly the effects of the war – will in itself be an explanation of why Nicholas was blamed. Better answers would demonstrate links between Nicholas and the problems; mistakes he made (such as personally taking over as commander of the army, leaving the government in the hands of his wife and Rasputin) or the inadequacies of his personality.

(b)	'The Provisional Government was overthrown because it decided to continue fighting in the First World War.' Do you agree with this statement about the revolution of November 1917? Give reasons for your answer.	15

Examiner's tip This question is testing your understanding of **causes** – the reasons why events occur. The number of marks available is a clear indication that you are expected to analyse this topic in some depth. To do this you need to be aware of the elements in the question so that you can build your answer around them.

1. You are given one cause for the overthrow of the Provisional Government, but you must not limit yourself to this. You must consider other possibilities. Were there other causes? If so, were they more or less important than continuing the war? Can any **single** cause be to blame? Don't all events have many causes? How do different causes link together?
2. You are free to agree or disagree with the statement in the question. The examiner is not looking for a **right** answer, what matters is the way you support your argument using relevant and accurate knowledge of the events.
3. Your answer must be about causes; don't feel that you have to write down everything you know about the November Revolution. You are being asked to analyse why events happened, and not to describe those events. On the other hand, do not think you can give a satisfactory answer without using your factual knowledge. Answers such as the following, which deal with causes but almost ignore the historical context, get very few marks.

> You can't say that there is just one reason for the overthrow of the Provisional Government. All events have many causes, and so did this, so although the war was important it does not on its own explain what happened. It was necessary for bringing about a situation in which the Government could be overthrown, but without other long-term and short-term causes the Government might have survived.

Examiner's tip Weak answers to this question will not consider the variety of possible causes. They might, for instance, agree with the statement in the question, and fail to consider other factors at all. Let's take a good answer and analyse the steps it takes in constructing an argument.

> Continuing the war was obviously a factor in the failure of the Provisional Government. Military defeat had played a great part in the overthrow of the Tsar, and the Provisional Government met the same fate. Once the new offensives ordered by Kerensky had failed, there were mass desertions, and the army almost disintegrated. The people could see

Answers to Unit 4

Question	Answer	Mark

no end to the suffering they were expected to put up with. The same factors for revolution existed in November as had existed in March.

Examiner's tip: The first paragraph establishes that the war was **one important factor** in the overthrow of the Provisional Government.

However, the war was not the only reason for the Government's failure. Its authority was undermined from the start by the influence of the Soviets over the soldiers and workers. The Petrograd Soviet was almost like another government in Russia. So the Provisional Government was never fully in control. As military failures continued, so the power of the Soviets increased. There were many people who were working to overthrow the Government. The Bolsheviks were only one of many revolutionary groups, but their influence in the Soviets steadily grew until they controlled many of them. Their propaganda, in particular their slogan 'Peace, Bread and Land', did much to undermine the Government by promising people what they most wanted. In Lenin, the Bolsheviks had a leader who was both capable and determined. By November, the Bolsheviks were ready to seize power.

Examiner's tip: The above paragraph shows that there were **other factors**, apart from the war, which weakened the Provisional Government.

When the Bolsheviks took power in the November Revolution, almost nobody was prepared to defend the Provisional Government. Like the Tsar's government in March, it collapsed easily. But even though the Bolsheviks were well organized and determined, it is hard to see how they could possibly have seized power without the chaos brought by the war. It is true that the Provisional Government had failed to solve any of the problems they inherited from the Tsar. Many of the ministers were wealthy or middle class, and they did not want the sweeping social reforms that Russia needed. The war made it easier for the revolutionaries to seize power – in March the Provisional Government had come to power almost by accident – but it was not the war which caused all of Russia's problems. Terrible poverty in the towns and in the countryside, when added to defeat in war, meant that most of Russia's people had little faith left in any government. So although the war was a major cause of the overthrow of the Provisional Government, I also think that other factors, both long and short term, helped to create a revolutionary situation in Russia in November 1917.

Examiner's tip: The final paragraph shows **links** between causes, discusses the **relative importance** of different causes and reaches a reasoned conclusion.

Answers to Unit 4

Question	Answer	Mark
2 (a)(i)	Study Source D. State what is meant by 'Bolshevik'.	1

Examiner's tip — As there is only one mark available, any correct identification would be sufficient. In the context of the source, Mikoyan is probably trying to praise the leader of the secret police by identifying him with the heroes of the Bolshevik revolution of 1917. However, in this question simply relating 'Bolshevik' to support for the Communist Party would be enough. The following answers would all score the mark.

(1) The Bolsheviks were the revolutionaries led by Lenin, who took over Russia in 1917. (2) Mikoyan meant that the leader of the secret police was a loyal supporter of the Communist government. (3) The word 'Bolshevik' in Source D means a member of the Soviet Communist Party.

(a) (ii)	Study Source D. What was the name of the secret police?	1

Examiner's tip — You need to be a little careful with this question, as the title of the Soviet secret police changed over the years. The correct answer for the date of this source is the NKVD. In fact, the Examiner decided also to allow earlier alternatives, such as the Cheka and OGPU, probably because Mikoyan was looking back at the work of the secret police over an unspecified period of time.

(b)	Study Source E. Give two 'enemies' which Communists felt were 'surrounding' them in the 1930s.	2

Examiner's tip — This question tests your comprehension of the source in the context of the period. There are lots of possible answers which the Examiner would accept as Kopelev's reference to enemies is not at all specific; it could mean enemies inside the Soviet Union, or other countries which were hostile to her. It could even mean other ideologies, such as fascism. But remember – the question asks for **two** enemies, so there will be one mark awarded for each. The following answer includes more than two acceptable points (but still only scores two marks!).

In the 1930s the Soviet Union felt that it had many enemies but it was particularly worried by the rise of fascism in countries like Germany and Italy. These two were certainly considered to be enemies. There were also enemies inside the Soviet Union, like the Trotskyists.

(c)	Study Source C. In what ways does this cartoon give a biased view of Trotsky? Explain your answer.	6

Examiner's tip — Bias is a concept which students do not deal with well. The almost universal assumption is that bias is a 'bad thing', which makes a source unreliable, if not useless. Of course, it is nothing of the sort. The bias of a source is nothing more than the perspective from which events are viewed; it does not have to be a deliberate distortion of the truth, although it can be. The different 'sides' taking part in an event will always have different views. For that matter, historians studying the same event often have different views as well. Most of History consists of opinions, judgements and interpretations of events, so we must not dismiss sources because they are biased; rather we should realise that they are bound to be biased, and that this makes them even more useful to us because it shows how people have perceived what happened in the past.

In this question, all you are asked to do is identify and explain the ways in which the source is biased against Trotsky. A good answer will use both the content of the cartoon (what it shows) as well as its provenance. The cartoon is obviously an

Answers to Unit 4

Question	Answer	Mark

unflattering image of Trotsky. The swastika hanging on the wall, and the German helmet full of blood, are intended to make it appear that Trotsky is working for the Germans. Trotsky is washing his hands in blood, which makes it appear that he is to blame for violence against the Soviet people. This is a Soviet cartoon from 1937, which puts forward the view of Trotsky which Stalin's government wanted the Soviet people to believe. An answer making these points would score highly.

The bias of this source is obviously against Trotsky. He is shown as a madman who is washing his hands in the blood of the Russian people. He is a kind of terrorist, as shown by all the weapons and bombs on the floor. Nobody who supported Trotsky would show him like this. The cartoon is really propaganda by Stalin's government, making Trotsky out to be a German spy. You can see this because of the German helmet that Trotsky is washing his hands in, and because of the swastika on the wall. At the time of the Purges Stalin was trying to make out that all his opponents were German spies.

(e) **Study Source A and Source B. Which of these two sources gives the more reliable explanation for the purging of ordinary people in the 1930s? Explain your answer by referring to both sources.** 8

Examiner's tip Questions like this one on the **reliability** of sources are used a lot in GCSE History papers. You are being asked whether or not you can believe what a source says or shows. A common trap to fall into is to judge the reliability of a source by its **type** – whether it is a cartoon, photograph, newspaper article etc.– so, for example, an answer might state that a cartoon must be unreliable because cartoons are drawn just to make people laugh; or that an eye-witness account must be reliable because the person saw what happened. These answers can never score many marks because they ignore **what the source actually says or shows**. Never limit your answers in this way. The **content** of a source is the most important single factor in helping you to decide whether the source is reliable. So, some cartoons are reliable and some are not; some eye-witnesses tell the truth and some do not. It all depends on what they say or show.

Having looked at the content of the source, then what? Unfortunately you cannot always believe what sources say. You need to take into account who produced a source and why they produced it. They might have wanted to mislead people, or persuade people to a certain point of view. Even when they told what they believed to be the truth, they might have given a version of the truth which was as favourable as possible to themselves. So, you must always doubt the accuracy of a source, and check elsewhere to test its reliability. There are two kinds of checks you can make. Firstly, do you have any other sources which say the same thing? This kind of checking is called cross-reference. The more sources you can find which agree with each other, the more likely it is (though still not certain) that they can be relied upon. The second check is against our own knowledge of events. It is surprisingly easy to forget this, given that it is the most obvious and important way of checking reliability that you have available to you.

The last point to make before we look at the two sources in this question is that a source can be reliable and unreliable at the same time. So, Source A may be telling lies about Afanasiya Uromova, and so would be unreliable as evidence of the supposed crimes she committed; but it would then be reliable as evidence of the way in which the Communist Party in Stalin's Russia persecuted its political opponents. In other words, the reliability of a source can only be judged in relation

Answers to Unit 4

Question	Answer	Mark

to the **purpose you have for it as evidence**. As it happens, this is not an issue in this particular question, as you are asked to judge the reliability of the sources as explanations of 'the purging of ordinary people in the 1930s', which limits the issue of reliability to this specific topic.

Good answers to this question, such as the following example, will evaluate each of the sources before reaching a conclusion.

> The problem with Source A is that people such as the local Communist Party Secretary might not have told the truth to the secret police. He could have been under pressure to report a certain number of people just to show he was not being lazy about identifying opponents of the Communist Party in his town; or he might just have had some personal grudge against Uromova. He would know that the secret police would probably arrest anybody that he reported because he was the local Party Secretary. On the other hand, even if what he says about Uromova is just made up, it still tells us the kinds of things that the Communist Party and the secret police would have regarded as crimes, because otherwise he would not have bothered making these accusations. It is obviously true, for instance, that anyone who had a portrait of Trotsky in their house would have been regarded as dangerous by the secret police, because Stalin saw Trotsky as his most bitter enemy. So, even if Source A is telling lies, it can still give us reasons why people were purged in the 1930s.
>
> Source B is taken from a novel, so you could say it is untrue and, therefore, unreliable as historical evidence. On the other hand, the writer had worked in the USSR as a journalist so he was in a position to gain first-hand information on events. The problem with this is that the Soviet government would probably only have allowed him to work in the USSR if they thought that he was sympathetic towards them. However, what he wrote in this source is not particularly sympathetic, because he is saying that people were shot just for not working enough, but adds that this was necessary if Russia was to modernise quickly. It's hard to see that the government would justify the Purges in this way — they claimed that the Purges were all about protecting Russia from its enemies. So the writer is not just giving the government view, and this probably makes what he says more reliable. Furthermore, given that Russia was modernising very fast in this period, what is said about the way in which the peasants had to adjust to a new way of life is true.
>
> Despite the fact that there are reasons for doubting what both Sources A and B say, they do give us a reasonable idea of the reasons why people were purged in the Soviet Union in the 1930s.

(e) **Study all the sources. 'The Purges of the 1930s only took place because Stalin feared Trotsky.' Do these sources provide reliable evidence to show this view to be true? Explain your answer fully.** 12

Examiner's tip
Here you have to use the sources to test whether or not a statement is true. Even though the question says 'Do these sources...*show* this view to be true?' you must not take the sources at face value — you must also judge the reliability of the sources as evidence for or against the given statement. You can

Answers to Unit 4

Question	Answer	Mark

hardly judge whether the statement is true before you have decided which evidence you can trust.

A common approach to this type of question is to take each source in turn and say whether or not it supports the statement. If you use this approach do not make the mistake of assuming that if more sources support the statement than oppose it, then it must be true. This would be to ignore the **quality** of evidence given by particular sources – some are more reliable, and more important, than others. The Examiner wants to see that you can evaluate the sources in order to select the evidence that is most persuasive. The specific conclusion you reach – whether Stalin's fear of Trotsky was the only reason for the Purges or not – does not matter. What counts is the way you use the evidence provided by the sources.

A good way to approach this question is to break the statement up into smaller, more manageable issues to explore. So here you could ask:
- Did Stalin fear Trotsky?
- Was Stalin's fear of Trotsky a reason for the Purges?
- Were there other reasons for the Purges?

In using the sources to cast light on each of these you will be answering the larger question originally set. Here is a particularly good example.

The sources give plenty of evidence that Stalin feared Trotsky. The best example is Source C, where the cartoon shows Trotsky as a German agent. This would never have been printed in 1937 without government approval, so it shows us how the government wished the Russian people to view Trotsky. The government would not have bothered with a piece of propaganda like this if Trotsky was unimportant. Another example of propaganda is Source D, where Mikoyan refers to Trotskyists as being enemies of the Communist state. Source E backs up the other two sources by confirming, in the author's memoirs, that Trotsky was used as a 'hate figure' by Stalin, even though many people did not really believe that Trotsky was a German agent. So, although what these sources say about Trotsky is completely unreliable – he was not a German agent – we can infer from them that Stalin saw Trotsky as a threat.

Examiner's tip | The first paragraph deals with the question 'Did Stalin fear Trotsky?'

What is less clear from these sources is whether Stalin's fear of Trotsky was a reason for the Purges. Certainly Trotskyists were regarded as enemies, but what is more likely is that Trotsky's name was just used as an excuse to persecute people. In Source A, for instance, the Party Secretary makes several accusations against Uromova. We cannot know if these accusations were true – there was such an atmosphere of terror at the time that the Secretary would know that he was dooming Uromova just by claiming she had a portrait of Trotsky in her house, but he could easily have had other reasons for wanting to get rid of her. Source E makes a similar point by saying that it did not really matter whether Trotsky was a German agent or not, but that, for the purposes of uniting the people, any opposition leader had to be presented as an enemy. In other words, Trotsky was an excuse for the Purges rather than a reason for them.

Answers to Unit 5

Question	Answer	Mark

Examiner's tip — The previous paragraph deals with the question 'Was Stalin's fear of Trotsky a reason for the Purges?'

> These sources do indicate that there were other reasons for the Purges. Source B is admittedly dubious in being an extract from a novel, written by someone who might have been a sympathiser with Stalin's government, but it does put the Purges into the context of what Stalin was doing to modernise Russia during the 1930s. It says that the Purges were necessary to force the people to accept the sacrifices needed during the Five Year Plans. This seems a plausible idea. Source E also fits the Purges into another context – the external threats faced by Russia in the 1930s. Kopelev's belief that the Purges were necessary to unite the Russian people against the enemies who surrounded them was shared by other Communists at the time.

Examiner's tip — This paragraph deals with the question 'Were there other reasons for the Purges?'

> In conclusion, these sources indicate that although Trotsky was a factor in the Purges, he was not the only factor. Stalin had many reasons for feeling threatened - and as an absolute dictator he would not tolerate opposition. He wanted Trotsky dead, and he later had him murdered; but fear of Trotsky was not the only reason for the Purges - in fact he was more an excuse for them than a reason.

5 THE UNITED STATES OF AMERICA, 1919–41

Question	Answer	Mark
1 (a)	**Study Sources A and B. What can you learn about the effects of the stock market crash of 1929 from these sources?**	3

Examiner's tip — This is a straightforward comprehension question. Only Source B makes direct reference to the stock market crash, but Source A seems to tell us about its effects.

Source A describes the predicament of an unemployed person, who previously worked in the construction industry, but is now reduced to begging. We can infer from it that the crash made people unemployed by reducing the amount of construction work being done. Source B is more direct in that it shows someone selling their car because they have lost all their money in the crash. It is possible to put the two sources together and make generalizations about the effects of the crash; that it put people out of work, that it made people desperate for money. Your answer does not need to be too detailed – as the small number of marks available on this question indicate – but you must make sure you use both sources, as in the following example.

Answers to Unit 5

Question	Answer	Mark

These sources show us how people were affected by the stock market crash, rather than telling us much about the crash itself. In Source A a beggar is remembering the work he did in the days before the crash. The source implies that there's no work any more, which shows that the crash made people unemployed and poor. It also shows that nobody was putting money into construction projects, or there would be jobs available. In Source B we can see someone who has lost all his money in the crash. He's so poor now that he has to sell his car to raise some money. Even though he looks quite well dressed he is obviously desperate for money. It shows us that the crash even affected people who were quite well-off beforehand.

(b) **Study Source B. How reliable is this source as evidence of the effects of the stock market crash? Explain your answer fully.** 4

> **Examiner's tip**
>
> In judging the reliability of a source we have to take a number of factors into consideration. First, make sure you accept the attribution of the source as the truth. Source B **does** show a scene in New York in October 1929. Never be tempted to question the source attribution; if you were permitted to do so, every question would be unanswerable.
>
> Next, look at the content of the source, and think about its reliability in the light of what you know about the topic. Source B shows a man selling his car because (he claims) he has lost all his money on the stock market. The photograph was taken in the month when the crash started, so it is possible that his claim is true. But there are other possibilities – he could, for instance, be claiming to have lost his money in order to attract the sympathy of potential buyers. We cannot prove this one way or the other, and the man's motives for selling the car obviously affect the nature of the source's reliability as evidence about the crash.
>
> Another question which arises is, even if the man has lost his money in the crash, how **typical** was he? Were many other people affected in the same way, or was this man unusual? You might even ask whether the photograph could have been taken **before** the crash – we know it was taken in October, but the crash did not start until 'Black Thursday', 24 October. Even in prosperous times some people are unfortunate enough to lose all their money on the stock market.
>
> Finally, we could question the motives of the photographer; why did he take the photograph? Perhaps he took it because the scene was so unusual, in which case it can only be reliable as evidence of the effects of the crash on this man. There are, then, lots of ways in which you can question this source's reliability. One way in which you should **not** judge the reliability of Source B, or any other source, is solely on the basis of its source **type**. The fact that Source B is a photograph does not affect its reliability; what matters is what the source shows. The following is a good example of how to raise issues of reliability.

Source B is probably reliable as evidence of how the crash affected some people. Lots of people lost their money in the crash, and the man in the photo could be one of these. The date of the photo fits well with the time of the crash, October 1929, but if it was taken before 24 October, when the crash began, then obviously it cannot be about the crash at all. Although it is probably reliable, we cannot be sure of this. For instance, we do not know that the man had lost his money. Maybe he wanted to sell his car for another reason, and he just wanted people to sympathize with him. We do not know why the photographer took this picture. It could have been such an unusual

Answers to Unit 5

Question	Answer	Mark

sight that this man was not at all typical of the way people were affected by the crash, and that's why the photographer was interested in him. If this is true, the photograph does not give a reliable impression of the effects of the crash.

(c) (i) Study Sources C and D. In what ways do these sources show the differing attitudes of Hoover and Roosevelt about the 'duties of the state'?   3

> **Examiner's tip** This is a comprehension and comparison question. The two statements put forward different political philosophies. All this question requires you to do is summarize the different points of view.

Hoover, the Republican, believes that the government should be involved as little as possible in the economic life of the nation. He thinks that if the government becomes involved, the effect is to undermine 'individual initiative', which is what makes the country wealthy. He sees government action as socialism. Roosevelt, the Democrat, has a different view. He thinks there are times when the government must become involved. In particular, the state must protect those who are not capable of looking after themselves.

(ii) Using Sources C and D and your own knowledge, how would you explain these differences?   5

> **Examiner's tip** The instruction to use your own knowledge applies both to explaining the different political viewpoints of Hoover and Roosevelt, and why they made these statements when they did. The Republicans and the Democrats represented different social groups. The Republicans were the party of the rich and of big business, so naturally they did not want the government interfering in their affairs. The Democrats represented the poor and the underprivileged, so naturally they were more sympathetic to the idea of using the power of the state to improve people's lives. Hoover's and Roosevelt's statements express these two different philosophies. However, the dates on the two sources are also significant. In 1928, before the crash, it made sense for Hoover to talk about the virtues of individual initiative, because the economy was still doing well. There was little need for the government to become more involved. But in 1932, when Roosevelt was speaking, millions were unemployed, and Americans were looking to the government for help. In addition, this speech was made during an election campaign, so naturally Roosevelt would tend to say what he thought the people wanted to hear. Your answer must make use of both the sources, and your knowledge, as the question requires. The following example does this well.

Hoover and Roosevelt were members of different political parties, and their statements summarize the philosophies of these parties. The Republicans believed in 'rugged individualism', and not the power of the state. This is because they were the party of the rich, who were doing well and did not want the government to change things. Hoover was a businessman himself, and strongly believed in free enterprise. The Democrats believed that the government had a duty to care for all

Answers to Unit 5

Question	Answer	Mark

citizens, and should pass laws and raise taxes to do this when necessary. They stood up for the poorer sections of society. Actually once the Depression started Hoover's government was forced to get involved in the economy, but in 1928 when he made the speech in Source C the economy was still doing quite well so he could still believe in his own philosophy. Equally, Roosevelt's speech was made in 1932 when he was standing for election as President, so he was bound to promise what people wanted. If he had been speaking in 1928 he might have agreed with some of the things that Hoover said.

(d) **Study all the sources. Do these sources provide enough evidence for you to say why there was a stock market crash in the USA in 1929? Explain your answer with reference to the sources.** 5

> **Examiner's tip**
> When a question asks whether you have **enough** evidence in the sources for a particular purpose, your first task is to see whether the sources contain **any** such evidence. Only when you have done this can you move on to making a judgement as to whether your evidence is sufficient for the purpose.
>
> These sources contain little direct evidence on the **causes** of the crash. Sources A, B and D are about the **effects** of the crash, so can almost be ignored. It is possible to infer some causes from Sources C and E (and maybe B), but there are clearly many areas relating to the causes of the crash that are not mentioned at all, such as the agricultural depression and industrial overproduction. Your answer needs to summarize the evidence these sources provide and then indicate that this is obviously not sufficient to explain the crash, as in the following example.

Some of these sources cover issues relating to causes of the crash, but they do not deal with the causes directly at all. Source B mentions losses on the stock market. Unrestricted speculation on the stock market was a cause of the crash, but Source B does not say this. Source C shows that Hoover who was President at the time was reluctant to allow government intervention in the economy. Perhaps if he had intervened a bit more, maybe to control the stock market, then the crash would not have happened, or not been so bad, but again, Source C does not say that. Source E shows the rapid growth in the automobile industry in the 1920s. It is true that industry was producing too much by the end of the 1920s, and could not find new markets, which also helped cause the crash, but Source E deals with registrations which shows how many automobiles were bought, not how many were made, so all it really does is show that industry was expanding, which ought to be a good thing. The other sources deal with effects of the crash, not causes. So the sources do not give very much evidence about causes of the crash. They also leave out lots of important causes entirely. For instance, there is no mention of the problems of agriculture at all. I think these sources are not enough evidence to explain why there was a stock market crash in 1929.

| 2 | (a) | Study Source A. What is meant by 'the CCC'? | 2 |

Answers to Unit 5

Question	Answer	Mark

Examiner's tip The 2 marks indicate that little more than the mere identification of the letters is required.

> The letters stand for Civilian Conservation Corps. This was an organization set up during the New Deal to provide work in the countryside for unemployed young people.

Examiner's tip The above answer would be awarded the 2 marks; one for identifying the letters CCC, and one for a brief explanation of what it did.

(b) Study Source C. How would the instruction 'Buy something' help President Roosevelt's policies succeed?   2

Examiner's tip Again, the low number of marks indicates that a brief answer based on source comprehension is enough. The source is encouraging people to spend money. If people buy things, factories have to make things. To make things factories need workers, workers get paid, they spend their pay, so factories have to produce more, and so on. The New Deal was based on the idea that if people were put back to work, then the recovery would happen, and this notice expresses the same idea in a slightly different way. The following example would easily gain 2 marks.

> President Roosevelt wanted to solve the problem of unemployment. He believed that if the government spent lots of money on various projects, this would create jobs. The workers on these projects would then have money to spend, and by spending it they would help to create more jobs. Source C was put on the wall of a company by its owner. When he told his workers to 'buy something', he understood Roosevelt's ideas. The more people spent, the more jobs there would be, and the more the country would recover from the Depression.

(c) Study Source D. In what ways would this graph be useful to an historian studying the New Deal? Explain your answer.   6

Examiner's tip The simplest answers to this question will assume that the source is useful because it tells us how many people were unemployed throughout the years of the New Deal; in other words, a source is useful for what it says or shows. This is true, but limited, and would not earn high marks.

Other answers might assume that because the source is **reliable**, it must be **useful**. This would rest on the notion that the graph is bound to be accurate, and indeed the attribution gives no reason to doubt it. The problem with such answers is that they are ignoring the question asked.

The best answers will be based on **inferences** which can be made using the graph; in other words, the graph is useful because the information it contains helps historians to reach conclusions or make judgements about the New Deal, e.g. on whether or not the New Deal was successful. The following is a good example of this approach.

> Whether a source is useful or not depends on what you want to use it for. This graph shows how many people were unemployed in the years

Answers to Unit 5

Question	Answer	Mark

during the New Deal, so it is not useful, for instance, in telling us about the work done by the New Deal agencies. However, we can use it to make some judgements about the New Deal. Roosevelt wanted to reduce unemployment. The graph shows he was successful to some extent, because after he came to power in 1933 unemployment did drop, but on the other hand, he did not really solve the problem, because even in the best year after 1933 unemployment only dropped to around 7 million. It was only when the war broke out in 1941 that unemployment reduced rapidly. We can say, then, that the graph is useful in showing that the New Deal was only a limited success.

(d) Study Source B and Source E. Which of these two views of the results of the New Deal is the more reliable? Explain your answer.   8

> **Examiner's tip** Reliability depends on many factors: When was the source produced? Who produced it? Why did they produce it? Sources can be reliable and unreliable at the same time; it all depends on how they are being used as evidence. A source might be a lie, and therefore unreliable in what it says, but reliable as evidence that its author is a liar. In this question we have to judge the reliability of two sources as evidence on the results of the New Deal.

There are reasons to doubt the reliability of each source as evidence on the effects of the New Deal. The cartoon shows Uncle Sam (representing the US government) with his arms round employers and workers. They are united, working together in the National Recovery Administration. The cartoon presents a positive image of the effects of the New Deal, it shows nothing of the opposition to the New Deal from employers, or indeed that the Supreme Court found the NRA unconstitutional in 1935. Its view of the effects of the New Deal is therefore biased towards the government. It is almost certainly taken from a newspaper which supported Roosevelt. Source E raises other kinds of doubts. Louis Banks was interviewed a long time after the events he describes. He had no reason to lie but there might be doubts about the accuracy of his memory. More important, his account states that the New Deal brought no benefit to him; it was only when the war came that he found employment by joining the army. But we know that many unemployed people did find work because of the New Deal, as Source D shows. So Louis Banks' experience tells us nothing of the successes of the New Deal, only that not everyone was helped by it. However, in this limited sense, it can be reliable, since it is consistent with the facts as we know them, and as they are shown on Source D. Source B is really just propaganda in favour of the New Deal, but Source E is probably reliable in what it says.

> **Examiner's tip** The above answer takes each source in turn and illustrates its weaknesses as evidence on the effects of the New Deal, using background knowledge and crossreference to another source to assess reliability, before reaching a conclusion. Any answer which does this will score highly.

Answers to Unit 5

Question	Answer	Mark
(e)	Study *all* the sources. 'The New Deal was not successful in restoring prosperity.' Do these sources show this view is true? Explain your answer fully.	12

Examiner's tip — There are two points to make about this type of question. First, do not take what the sources say at face value. You have to judge the reliability of the sources before you can decide whether or not they support the statement. Second, the sources will probably offer some evidence both for and against the statement. You need to consider both sides of the argument before reaching a conclusion, as in the following example.

> The sources do give some support to the view that the New Deal did not restore prosperity. In Source A it shows that one unemployed person could not find a proper job, but had to keep going back to the CCC for employment. If the New Deal had been working he would not have had to do this. A similar thing is shown in Source E where another person unemployed throughout the 1930s says that it was only when the war started that he was able to find a job by joining the army. It is true that both these sources were from interviews in 1970, so their memories might not have been all that clear, but there is no real reason to doubt what they said. Source D shows that unemployment remained high during the 1930s so it is hard to see that prosperity could have returned.

Examiner's tip — The first paragraph summarizes the evidence in support of the statement.

> On the other hand some of the sources do show that the New Deal improved things. Source B shows employers and workers cooperating in the NRA. They seem very positive and purposeful, which indicates that the government was helping to put industry back on its feet. The problem is that this source is so obviously supporting the government that it is hard to be sure that it is giving an accurate picture. It says nothing, for instance, about the way many employers opposed the New Deal. Source C shows that Roosevelt had some supporters, but as it is from 1933 it cannot tell us anything about whether the New Deal succeeded in bringing back prosperity; it is more about how the New Deal hoped to bring back prosperity. Source D does show some success for the New Deal particularly in the years up to 1937. It is unrealistic to think that anyone could find jobs for all the unemployed, but over four years Roosevelt reduced unemployment by around 5 million, which did quite a lot to restore prosperity.

Examiner's tip — The second paragraph summarizes the evidence against the statement.

> Overall, these sources do not give much evidence to suggest that the New Deal restored prosperity in America. There is more evidence to suggest that it did not. A lot depends on what counts as 'restoring prosperity'. The New Deal certainly made things better, even though it

Answers to Unit 5

Question	Answer	Mark

did not restore America to the prosperity it had enjoyed before the Depression.

Examiner's tip The final paragraph states the conclusion reached by considering all the evidence.

---

6 EVENTS IN THE 1930s LEADING TO THE SECOND WORLD WAR

Question	Answer	Mark

1 (a) Has this map any value for a study of German expansion in the years 1936–9?   5

Examiner's tip This question asks you to use your knowledge of the period to identify how some of the features on the map help explain German expansion. However, it is also important to note where the map comes from (a German atlas published in 1936), which means that it reflects German attitudes. In fact, the areas marked as 'German Speaking Territory' and 'German Culture Territory' give us the German justification for their policy of expansion. You need to bring together in your answer what you can learn from the map and your knowledge of the relevant events between 1936 and 1939. These events should include the *Anschluss* with Austria in 1938, the taking of the Sudetenland in 1938 and the invasion of Czechoslovakia and Poland in 1939. You can then explain how the map has some value for studying German expansion during this period, but you may argue that its value is limited for understanding Hitler's actions, as the following answer does.

This map has some value because it shows the areas which the Germans thought should be part of a Greater Germany. Hitler thought that the Treaty of Versailles had split German people off from each other into different countries. He complained this meant there were many Germans living under the rule of other countries against their will. He wanted to unite all Germans in the same country. He also wanted more land in the east for Germany's growing population. The map shows that these 'German' areas include Austria, Czechoslovakia and parts of Poland. Almost all these areas were taken over by Germany between 1936 and 1939. There were 8 million German speakers living in Austria. Many people agreed that they should be allowed to join with Germany although the Treaty of Versailles banned it. After the German army had marched into Austria the Austrians voted to unite with Germany. In 1938 Hitler claimed that the Czech government was mistreating the many Germans living in the Sudetenland. Chamberlain thought it was reasonable for the Sudetenland to be given to Germany because most of the people there were Germans. This is shown on the map, but the map also shows there was not much justification for invading the rest of Czechoslovakia. The map also shows that the land dividing the two parts of Germany was also full of Germans. But the map does not

Answers to Unit 6

Question	Answer	Mark

explain why Hitler wanted the rest of Poland. He wanted this as 'living space' for Germany to grow. So the map explains some of the German expansion between 1936–9, but not all of it.

(b) **By October 1938 both Austria and the Sudetenland area of Czechoslovakia had become part of Germany. Did Germany use the same methods to gain control of these two areas? Explain your answer.** 8

> **Examiner's tip** Of course, it is not enough simply to say, 'No, Germany used different methods.' You must clearly identify and explain the differences and the similarities. Let's look at the differences first.
>
> 1 The occupation of Austria was completed without the agreement of other countries, while Hitler gained the agreement of Britain and France for the occupation of the Sudetenland.
> 2 Hitler persuaded the leader of Austria to ask for German troops to enter the country, while the leader of Czechoslovakia opposed German occupation.
> 3 Before the takeover, Hitler managed to replace the Austrian Chancellor with a Nazi who would do what he was told. He did not do this in Czechoslovakia.
> 4 Hitler claimed that German troops were sent into Austria to help the government stop a plot and restore order, while he claimed they were sent into the Sudetenland to protect Germans already living there.
> 5 In Austria Hitler let the people vote; in the Sudetenland they were not given this opportunity.
>
> To achieve high marks, you will need first to identify the differences, i.e. explain what happened in both countries and how this differed. Do not just say what happened in one, leaving it to the examiner to guess that what you mean is that this method was not used in the other country, e.g. 'The difference is that the leader of Austria asked Hitler to send troops in.' Second, use your knowledge of the events briefly to explain the differences. For example, instead of writing that no other countries agreed to the occupation of Austria, whereas they did agree to occupation of the Sudetenland; explain the importance of the Munich meetings, what was agreed and who was present. Now turn to the similarities. These might include:
>
> 1 In both cases Hitler used intimidation and the German army to back up his actions and claims.
> 2 In both cases he used the Nazi Party within the country to be occupied, thus giving him his excuse to go in.
> 3 In both cases he used the argument that there were many Germans living in the country who wanted to live under German rule.
>
> Don't worry, you will not be expected to cover all these similarities and differences. You don't have the time. A couple of each will be enough for a good mark. Look at the following two answers. Which do you think is better?

1   *Hitler used completely different methods. In one he got other countries to agree before he marched in, but in the other he got the Nazis there to stir up trouble to give him an excuse to go in. In one of them he gave the people a choice, but in the other he didn't give them a choice.*

2   *He used a mixture of the same and different methods. In both he used the justification that the people there were Germans so they should be living under German rule. In both he got the local Nazi party to stir*

Answers to Unit 6

Question	Answer	Mark
	up trouble first. But in Austria he first managed to get a Nazi Chancellor appointed (Seyss-Inquart). He invited the German army in to help deal with the disorders (which were caused by the Nazi Party under Hitler's instructions). So Hitler was in league with some of the Austrians. Because of this he did not need international agreement. The Czechoslovakian President Benes would not agree to what Hitler wanted. So Hitler used different tactics. He claimed that the Germans there were being mistreated by the government and got France and Britain at Munich to agree to the Sudetenland becoming German if he promised to leave the rest of Czechoslovakia alone. So in Austria he had no international agreement but agreement from within, in the Sudetenland he had international agreement but no agreement from the government.	
(c)	**How did the attitudes of the British and French governments towards German actions change in 1939?**	6
	Examiner's tip This question is asking you to explain **how** attitudes changed, and not why. It is therefore best to explain first what British and French attitudes were at the beginning of 1939 and then describe the changes which took place. The following answer does this in a straightforward way. It is perfectly adequate for a high mark.	
	At the beginning of 1939 the British and the French governments still believed in appeasement as can be seen by their agreement in 1938 at Munich to let Hitler have the Sudetenland. They were sure they were saving Europe from war. They also believed that there was nothing wrong with all Germans being able to live together in the same country. They also probably saw Hitler as a defence against the Communists in Russia. They did not see Hitler as a threat to them. Chamberlain also realized that Britain was not yet ready to fight a war. Since 1936 Britain had been rearming, but Chamberlain still thought Hitler could be trusted. But after the invasion of Czechoslovakia in March 1939 the British and French realized that Hitler was not going to stop there and that Poland might be next on the list. They realized Hitler was a threat to them and that it was worth fighting to defend Poland because this might stop a larger war later. Britain and France promised to protect Poland's independence, which eventually took them into the war when Germany invaded Poland. So their attitudes had changed a lot.	
(d)	**From the time that Hitler came to power in 1933 Germany and the Soviet Union fought a war of words. Yet in August 1939 the Soviet Union signed a pact with Germany. Why did the Soviet Union take this action?**	6

Answers to Unit 7

Question	Answer	Mark

Examiner's tip This question differs from (c) because it asks **why** rather than **how**. Why did the Soviet Union sign the pact with Germany? At first sight, this does seem a surprising thing for the Soviet Union to have done. But as this answer explains, Stalin had good reasons for his actions. Note that the answer gives more than one reason.

> Stalin was worried when Britain and France gave in to Hitler over the Sudetenland. He thought they were keeping Hitler happy so he would not attack them. They hoped he would turn eastwards instead and attack Russia. Stalin felt Russia was left isolated to face Germany. Stalin had to look after his country and so he agreed to the Pact. It had great advantages for Russia. Russia would get part of Poland, and Russia would be safe from Germany. It also gave Russia some time in which to improve its defences. Stalin thought he could doublecross Hitler later when he was ready. The trouble was Hitler doublecrossed him first.

7 THE COLD WAR

Question	Answer	Mark
1 (a)	Study Source A. Explain in your own words why, according to this source, Marshall Aid was introduced.	3

Examiner's tip This is a comprehension exercise. The question instructs you to explain the reasons given **in the source** for the introduction of Marshall Aid, so make sure your answer is derived from the source; you are not being asked to answer from your own background knowledge. Include in your answer all the relevant material you can extract from the source, and **use your own words**, do not just copy out the source. Given the small number of marks available you can be sure that any reasonable summary, as in the following example, will score highly.

> The source says that Marshall Aid was introduced so that the world's economy could be rebuilt. It was a time when the world was suffering from lots of problems after the war. Aid was needed to prevent people from starving, and to restore order and prosperity.

(b)	Study Sources A and B. In what ways do these sources show differing attitudes towards the Marshall Plan?	3

Examiner's tip When you are asked to identify differences between sources, you should be aware that some differences will be more obvious than others. Some differences will be explicit – the sources will state different things. Other differences will be implicit – you will need to infer them from what is said. So here Source A says that the Marshall Plan is not directed 'against any country or doctrine', but Source B says the Plan is 'just another version of the Truman Doctrine', which means that it is directed against Communism.

71

Answers to Unit 7

Question	Answer	Mark

> This is a clear, explicit difference. However, if we were to say that Source A is in favour of the Marshall Plan and Source B is against it, we would be **inferring** a difference between them, because the sources do not actually state this difference.
>
> When writing your answer, include any explicit differences you can spot, but also be aware of opportunities to make inferences. The following example is brief (the question only carries 3 marks), but is sufficient to earn full marks.

Marshall is obviously in favour of the Plan and Vyshinsky is against it. The Russians think the Plan is antiSoviet, that's why they compare it to the Truman Doctrine and say that it will limit freedom of choice, and the Americans are trying to pretend it isn't by saying it's not directed against anybody, and they are just trying to rebuild the world economy.

(c) Using Sources A and B, and your own knowledge, how would you explain the differences between these two sources? — 5

> **Examiner's tip** The important instruction here is to use both your own knowledge and material from the sources. You will not score full marks if you use only one or the other. The following example shows how to use both.

The basic difference between the two sources is that one is for the Marshall Plan and one is against. Marshall's statement describes what the Plan might achieve – preventing hunger, poverty, and helping the world's economy to recover – but from the Soviet side this looked very different. They thought it was just a way for the Americans to increase their power and influence, hence the reference to the Truman Doctrine. Marshall's claim that the Plan was not directed against any country might have been true, but it isn't surprising that the Soviets did not agree.

> **Examiner's tip** The first paragraph explains the differences in the sources.

Of course, the Soviets probably would not have been worried about the Marshall Plan if they had been friendly with the USA. But this was the time of the Cold War. The Americans were using Marshall Aid as a means of stopping the spread of Communism, and the USSR understood this, and opposed it. This is what accounts for the differences in attitudes to Marshall Aid shown in the two sources.

> **Examiner's tip** The second paragraph explains the differences using background knowledge.

(d) Study Sources A, B and C. How useful are Sources A, B and C for understanding the purposes of the Marshall Plan? Explain your answer by reference to the sources. — 4

Answers to Unit 7

Question	Answer	Mark

Examiner's tip — Sources are useful for the evidence they provide to historians. Be careful not to take what a source says at face value. Here, as in all questions about the usefulness of sources, you need to look beneath the surface meaning. Can you really believe what Marshall says about the purposes of the Plan? He is bound to present the Plan in a favourable light, and he might have good reasons for not being entirely honest about its purposes. On the other hand, Vyshinsky is stating the Soviet view of the purposes of the Plan. You might even wish to question what the British historian has to say, although Source C has no obvious bias. In evaluating the sources you will need to judge what they say in the light of your own knowledge – do they agree or disagree with the facts as you know them?

Answers which just treat the sources as information, and take them at face value, will not score a high mark. Answers like the following one, which show a willingness to question the reliability of the sources, and to comment on how this affects their usefulness, would certainly achieve all 4 marks.

Source A says that the Marshall Plan was all about solving problems of hunger and poverty, and rebuilding the world's economy, but this is Marshall himself saying this. Of course, the USA did give a huge amount of aid to many countries, but we cannot be sure about why they did this. The Russians obviously thought that its purpose was to stop the spread of Communism, because Source B compares it to the Truman Doctrine. If this was its purpose Marshall probably would not say so, because it would not make the USA look as good, and he probably wanted Communist countries to take the aid as well so that they would be tied to the USA. In a way Source C supports what Source B says because it shows that Britain did cooperate with the USA. So although these sources disagree in what they say about the purposes of the Plan, they are useful in showing different opinions on what the Plan was for.

(e) **Study Sources C, D and E. Do these sources provide you with enough evidence to explain how the Marshall Plan was put into operation in Europe? Explain your answer with reference to the sources.** 5

Examiner's tip — The sources do provide **some** evidence on how the Plan was put into operation. However, the question is asking whether this evidence is **enough**. Obviously, it is highly unlikely that three sources would be sufficient to explain all you need to know about the operation of the Marshall Plan. A good answer here will indicate what evidence the sources provide, and then indicate its limitations. Again, remember that you can **infer** evidence from sources as well as simply using what they say or show. The following example does all of these.

Source C says that the Plan was put into operation speedily, and that Britain played an important part in organizing it. Source D shows that goods were imported into Europe for distribution as Marshall Aid, but as it was not delivered until 1948, and the Plan was announced in June 1947, it can't have been organized all that quickly. Source E shows the countries which received aid under the Plan. None of them were Communist countries which shows that the Russians were successful in preventing the Americans from using the Plan to spread

Answers to Unit 7

Question	Answer	Mark

their influence in eastern Europe. The amount of aid was huge, and must have been a tremendous help to western Europe in recovering from the war. However, these three sources cannot give you all the evidence you would need to explain how the Plan was put into operation. For instance, in Source E we don't know how much each country received, in Source C it talks about organizing the Plan but it doesn't tell us who decided what goods should be given to different countries, and in Source D we don't know who is going to receive the sugar. These are just examples of what the sources don't tell you.

2 (a) (i) Name the leader of the USSR who attended the Yalta Conference in 1945.   **1**

Stalin.

(ii) Explain what is meant by the 'Truman Doctrine'. *Briefly* **use your knowledge of the USA's policy towards Communism between 1945 and 1955 to support your answer.**   **3**

Examiner's tip: Do not ignore the instruction to keep your answer brief. The examiner is helping you by indicating that a brief answer will be enough. Define the Truman Doctrine and then give one or two examples to illustrate how it was used. The following answer would certainly receive full marks, and shows just how brief a good answer can be.

In 1947 President Truman of the USA issued this doctrine. It stated that the USA would give help to any country threatened by Communist takeover. It applied in Greece, and led to Communist defeat in the Civil War. You could also say it applied in the Korean War.

(b) How *similar* were the following to each other:

I   The Yalta Conference;
II The Potsdam Conference?   **6**

Examiner's tip: There were similarities between the two conferences and you should be able to give some. However, the key words in this question are 'How similar'; this indicates that you must make some kind of judgement and that you need to consider differences as well as similarities before reaching your conclusion. Given that there are only 6 marks available, you would only have to mention a few similarities and differences – a lengthy comparison is not required, as the following example illustrates.

Yalta and Potsdam were both conferences of the victorious allies. The two conferences were similar in many important ways because they were both dealing with problems that had to be solved as the war came to an end. For instance, they both were concerned with how Germany was to be treated – Potsdam confirmed the decision made at Yalta to split Germany into zones of occupation. They both discussed Poland's frontiers, fixing its western frontier on the Oder-Neisse line. However, in

Answers to Unit 7

Question	Answer	Mark

other respects they were totally different. The atmosphere at Yalta was much more cooperative than that at Potsdam. Roosevelt was still alive at Yalta, and he was determined to get on with Stalin, but at Potsdam the USA was represented by Truman who was antiCommunist and much more suspicious of Stalin. In fact, Stalin was the only leader who attended both conferences, as Churchill was replaced by Attlee for the Potsdam Conference. By the time of Potsdam the Cold War had really begun, whilst at Yalta the allies were still able to cooperate because the war against Germany was still continuing. So Yalta and Potsdam were similar in the issues they had to consider, but quite different in the attitudes of the allies towards each other.

(c) **Which *one* of the following was the most important reason why relations became very poor between the USSR and the USA by 1955:**

    I   the 'Iron Curtain';
    II the division of Germany;
    III Marshall Aid?

Explain your answer fully by referring to I, II and III.   15

> **Examiner's tip** This question asks you to analyse the causes of hostility between the USSR and the USA in the early years of the Cold War. All of the given causes were important, but the question tells you to choose the one you think was the most important and to explain your choice. To do this you must not only show why your chosen cause was important, you must demonstrate why it was **more** important than the others, and why the others were **less** important than your choice. This means you must **compare** the importance of the given causes. The following example shows you how to construct an answer which covers all these points.

Each of the three causes helped to create bad relations between the USSR and the USA. The creation of an 'Iron Curtain' by the USSR after 1945 by taking over most of the countries in eastern Europe, and forcing the people in those countries to have Communist governments, made the USA certain that the Communists had to be resisted or they would just take over more countries. Splitting Germany into four zones also caused problems because the Soviet Union had different plans for Germany compared with the other allies. The USSR used the eastern zone as a kind of colony – they just wanted to grab what they could to help build up their own economy and pay for war damage, and they didn't want Germany to recover from the war. The western allies soon decided that allowing Germany to recover would be a good idea, as it would be protection against Communist expansion. These disagreements came to a head during the Berlin crisis in 1948–9. Finally Marshall Aid also caused hostility because the USSR suspected the USA's motives, and saw the Plan as just another way of spreading American influence in Europe.

> **Examiner's tip** The first paragraph shows how each cause was important in causing bad relations between the USSR and the USA.

However, out of these three causes the Iron Curtain was the most

Answers

important. The Marshall Plan was a reaction to Communist expansion, so it might not have been needed if the USA wasn't already worried by the creation of the Iron Curtain. The decision to split Germany was made while the Allies were still all getting on reasonably well together during the war, so if suspicion over the creation of the Iron Curtain had not developed after the war, the issue of Germany would probably not have caused hostility.

> **Examiner's tip** The second paragraph shows why two causes were less important than the third.

So I think the Iron Curtain was the most important cause of bad relations. More than anything else Stalin's determination to dominate eastern Europe so that the USSR would be secure from future attack was what created the Cold War. Even at Yalta there were fears that he would not allow free elections in Poland, and these came rapidly true. Once the USA was convinced that Stalin was determined to spread Communism throughout eastern Europe, every issue became a dispute between the two countries. Quarrels over divided Germany and the Marshall Plan were just episodes in the Cold War that suspicions over the Iron Curtain had created.

> **Examiner's tip** The final paragraph shows why the chosen cause was more important than the others.